D1243834

Commodore Ellsworth P. Bertholf

LIBRARY OF NAVAL BIOGRAPHY

COMMODORE ELLSWORTH P. BERTHOLF

FIRST
Commandant
OF THE
Coast Guard

C. Douglas Kroll

NAVAL INSTITUTE PRESS
Annapolis, Maryland

Naval Institute Press
291 Wood Road
Annapolis, MD 21402

Library of Congress Cataloging-in-Publication Data
Kroll, C. Douglas.
    Commodore Ellsworth P. Bertholf : first Commandant of the Coast Guard
/ Douglas Kroll.
        p.   cm.— (Library of naval biography)
    Includes bibliographical references and index.
    ISBN 1-55750-474-1 (alk. paper)
    1. Bertholf, Ellsworth Price, b. 1866. 2. United States. Coast Guard—
Officers—Biography. I. Title. II. Series.
    V63.B484 K76 2002
    363.28'6'092—dc21
    [B]

                                                            2001059625

Printed in the United States of America on acid-free paper ∞
09 08 07 06 05 04 03 02   9 8 7 6 5 4 3 2
First printing

Frontispiece courtesy of Bertholf family

For my wife, Lana

❧ Contents ❧

ᐥ᪲ Foreword ᓓ᪲

Ellsworth P. Bertholf's name is largely unknown today, even in the U.S. Coast Guard, the sea service he headed at the time of its birth in 1915. No vessel or major facility has ever been named for him despite his illustrious career. Born in New York City and reared in New Jersey, he attended the Naval Academy in Annapolis but was dismissed for his involvement in a hazing incident. Determined to pursue a career at sea, young Bertholf entered the Revenue-Cutter Service School of Instruction and following graduation in 1887 embarked on the first of many tours of sea duty.

Bertholf's early career reflects the wide variety of duties assigned to the Revenue-Cutter Service during the late nineteenth century. Like other Revenue-Cutter Service officers, he enforced import duties and laws regulating fishing, sealing, and whaling; participated in daring sea rescues; endured long months patrolling the North Pacific; and administered justice in Alaska. Bertholf first achieved fame for his part in an expedition hundreds of miles across Alaska to rescue whalers trapped near Point Barrow during the winter of 1897—98. Congress recognized his achievement by ordering a gold medal struck in Bertholf's honor.

Four years later Bertholf met with Russian officials in Saint Petersburg, then crossed Russia overland to purchase Siberian reindeer and transport them across the Bering Sea to Alaska, where they formed the herds that became a mainstay of Inuit survival. Between these expeditions Bertholf gained administrative experience as an executive officer, experience he put to good use when he was attached to the Life-Saving Service for almost three years. That civilian service and the quasi-military Revenue-Cutter Service, separate arms of the Treasury Department, would be merged a decade later to form the Coast Guard.

In 1911 Bertholf became captain-commandant of the Revenue-Cutter

Service. While serving as the senior officer in the service, he helped orga-
nize an ice patrol to alert ships to the presence of icebergs such as the one
that sank the *Titanic,* represented the United States at the International
Maritime Conference held in London in 1913, and prepared the service for
participation in World War I. As in all conflicts since the Quasi-War with
France in 1798, the Revenue-Cutter Service was transferred from the
Department of the Treasury to the Department of the Navy for the duration of the hostilities. Bertholf skillfully resisted the navy's subsequent
attempt to absorb the Revenue-Cutter Service and effected its union with
the Life-Saving Service to form the new U.S. Coast Guard. Serving as the
first commandant of the new service, Bertholf knit the two organizations
into one before retiring in mid-1919. Ellsworth P. Bertholf died suddenly
just over two years later. His was a life of adventure, service, and achievement. It is surprising that it has not been told before. Douglas Kroll is well
prepared to write this first scholarly biography of Bertholf. Kroll graduated
from the U.S. Coast Guard Academy and served at sea before transferring
to the navy, where he became a chaplain. Retiring after a quarter century of
service, Kroll completed a Ph.D. in history and now teaches at the College
of the Desert in California. In this biography Kroll captures the character
both of his subject and of the Revenue-Cutter Service during its final years.
He provides insights into the formation of the new Coast Guard, but most
of all he tells a good story, tracing the life of a man of accomplishment and
zeal. In this biography Ellsworth Bertholf finally receives his due.

The Library of Naval Biography provides accurate, informative, and
interpretive biographies of influential naval figures—men and women
who shaped or reflected the naval affairs of their time. Each volume
explains the forces that acted on its subject as well as the significance of
that person in history. Some volumes explore the lives of individuals who
have not previously been the subjects of modern, full-scale biographies;
others reexamine the lives of better-known individuals, adding new
information, a differing perspective, or a fresh interpretation. The series
is international in scope and includes individuals from several centuries.
All the volumes are based on solid research and written for general readers as well as specialists.

   With these goals in mind, the length of each volume has been limited.
The notes are at the end of the text and are restricted primarily to source
references. A brief essay on "Further Reading" assesses previous biogra-

phies of the subject and directs readers to the most important studies of the era and events in which the person lived and participated. It is the intention that this combination of clear writing, fresh interpretations, and solid historical context will result in volumes that both restore the all-important human dimension to naval history and are enjoyable to read.

James C. Bradford
Series Editor

⤝ *Preface* ⤞

I first became interested in Ellsworth P. Bertholf while reading Robert Johnson's *Guardians of the Sea*. Johnson wrote that the Coast Guard's neglect of Bertholf "can only be categorized as shameful" and went on to argue that Bertholf should be ranked among the Coast Guard's greatest commandants. When I was searching for a dissertation topic, I remembered Johnson's comments about Bertholf and decided to investigate his life and career.

Bertholf never saw combat, but the hostile Arctic environments of Alaska, Siberia, the Arctic Ocean, and the Bering Sea were as dangerous as any Spanish warship during the Spanish-American War, or any German U-boat during World War I. He took great risks and overcame numerous challenges—most frequently for humanitarian missions—to help someone or a group of people in need. Even had Bertholf never become commandant he would have achieved a permanent place in the Coast Guard's history as a highly decorated hero of the overland relief expedition to Point Barrow, one of the nation's greatest peacetime rescues.

Bertholf is a key figure in the Coast Guard's history. As the final commandant of the Revenue-Cutter Service and the first commandant of the U.S. Coast Guard he is a singular link between the legacy of the past and the Coast Guard of today. Initially appointed by President William H. Taft, a Republican, he was reappointed to a second term by President Woodrow Wilson, a Democrat. As its first commandant, Bertholf played a central role in the formation of the Coast Guard. The origins of Coast Guard aviation trace back to Bertholf's administration, as does the International Ice Patrol. As a U.S. delegate to the first International Conference on the Safety of Life at Sea, Bertholf established a leadership role for the Coast Guard that has since expanded to a position of global leadership. He also led the Coast Guard through World War I, during which its personnel suffered the highest percentage of casualties of any U.S. armed force.

In many respects Bertholf is similar to Bvt. Maj. Archibald Henderson, the fifth commandant of the Marine Corps, who defeated efforts in 1830 to merge the Marine Corps with the U.S. Army or Navy and established the relationship between the navy and Marine Corps that exists today. Shortly after Bertholf became commandant of the Revenue-Cutter Service, a presidential commission recommended its abolition. Bertholf successfully fought to preserve his service by merging it with the Life-Saving Service to form the U.S. Coast Guard. At the end of World War I, an attempt was made to merge the newly created Coast Guard with the navy—a move that would have meant the end of the Coast Guard. Bertholf successfully averted that threat as well. The Coast Guard is as indebted to Bertholf as the Marine Corps is to Henderson. While Henderson's contribution is well known, Bertholf's is not.

⸙ *Acknowledgments* ⸙

I incurred many debts to individuals and institutions in writing this book. I owe a great debt to Harold W. Rood, who was the perfect adviser and mentor for my doctoral dissertation. He generously read and reread drafts and always provided excellent suggestions and on-target criticisms. I cannot imagine a more encouraging adviser and mentor.

Among the long list of archivists and librarians who aided my research I am especially grateful to Pamela McNulty, reference librarian at the U.S. Coast Guard Academy Library, New London, Connecticut; John VanDereedt and Rick Peuser at the National Archives; Robert M. Browning Jr. and Scott T. Price, historians at Coast Guard Headquarters, Washington, D.C.; Nancy Kervin at the Senate Library, Washington, D.C.; Gary LaValley at the William W. Jeffries Memorial Archives, U.S. Naval Academy, Annapolis, Maryland; Bob Griffin, president of the Bergen County Historical Society, Hackensack, New Jersey; Richard Lenk, the Hackensack city historian; and Raymond Bertholf, the Bertholf family genealogist, of Paramus, New Jersey. I am also grateful to Bob Douville for so generously sharing his research on Bertholf, as well as copies of photos he had gathered. Staff members at the New York City Public Library, the Los Angeles Public Library, the Hackensack Public Library, and the Honnold/Mudd Library of the Claremont Colleges also gave valuable assistance. Funding for the research and writing of this dissertation was provided in part by the Rear Admiral John D. Hayes Pre-doctoral Fellowship of the Naval Historical Center, Washington, D.C.

I also greatly appreciate the assistance of James Bradford, the series editor, and Melinda Conner, the copyeditor, for their suggestions in improving my writing style.

Finally, I am at a loss as to how adequately to express my debt to my wife, Lana, to whom I dedicate this work. Her steadfast emotional and physical support enabled me to finish this book.

~⋙ *Chronology* ⋘~

7 Apr. 1866	Born in New York City, New York
28 Sept. 1882	Appointed naval cadet, U.S. Naval Academy, Annapolis
12 Sept. 1883	Court-martialed; dismissed from Naval Academy
4 Sept. 1885	Appointed cadet, U.S. Revenue-Cutter Service, School of Instruction, New Bedford
18 Oct. 1887	Graduated from School of Instruction
Dec. 1887–Apr. 1890	Service aboard USRC *Levi Woodbury*
12 June 1889	Commissioned third lieutenant, U.S. Revenue-Cutter Service
Apr. 1890–May 1891	Service aboard USRC *William H. Seward*
May 1891–Oct. 1892	Service aboard USRC *Forward*
31 Oct. 1892	Promoted to second lieutenant, U.S. Revenue-Cutter Service
June 1893–May 1995	Service aboard USRC *Hamilton*
15 Oct. 1895	Graduated from U.S. Naval War College
Nov. 1895–Aug. 1897	Executive officer, USRC *Salmon P. Chase* and School of Instruction
Nov. 1897–Jan. 1899	Service aboard USRC *Bear;* overland expedition to Point Barrow
Mar.–May 1899	Service aboard USRC *Thetis*
May 1899–Jan. 1901	Executive officer, USRC *Bear*
18 June 1900	Promoted to first lieutenant, U.S. Revenue-Cutter Service
Jan. 1901–Jan. 1902	Expedition across Russia
Apr.–Nov. 1902	Executive officer, USRC *Manning*
6 Dec. 1902	Married Emilie Innes Sublett
Dec. 1902–Oct. 1905	Service with U.S. Life-Saving Service

Nov. 1905–Nov. 1906	Executive officer, USRC *Onondaga*
Nov. 1906–Sept. 1907	Commander of USRC *Wissahickon*
31 Aug. 1907	Promoted to captain, U.S. Revenue-Cutter Service
Sept.–Nov. 1907	Temporary commander of USRC *Seminole*
Dec. 1907–Dec. 1910	Commander of USRC *Bear*
Dec. 1910–June 1911	Commander of USRC *Morrill*
19 June 1911	Promoted to captain-commandant, U.S. Revenue-Cutter Service
19 June 1915	Appointed captain-commandant, U.S. Coast Guard
1 July 1918	Promoted to commodore, U.S. Coast Guard
30 June 1919	Retired from U.S. Coast Guard
July 1919–Nov. 1921	Vice president, American Bureau of Shipping
11 Nov. 1921	Died in New York City of natural causes

Commodore Ellsworth P. Bertholf

⁓❧ I ❧⁓

BOYHOOD

*T*he thirst for adventure that characterized the life of Ellsworth Price Bertholf was a function of both his heritage and his upbringing. Perhaps he got his adventuresome spirit from his father, John J. Bertholf, who in 1849, at the age of eighteen, left his home and family in New York City and with thousands of other young men traveled to California to seek his fortune in the gold rush. Like most of his fellow adventurers, John Bertholf discovered that the gold was not easy to obtain. When prospecting for gold failed to pan out, he secured a position as the assistant customs collector of the port of San Francisco and gained knowledge of accounting that he would later use to support his family.

After a few years he returned to New York City and obtained an appointment in the New York Custom House. John Bertholf married Mary Jane Williamson on 28 December 1853 and within a few years had two daughters: Frances Lavinia, born in September 1854, and Mary Eugene, born in April 1857. Tragedy struck less than a year after the birth of their second daughter when Mary Jane died on 17 February 1858. For three years John was a widower with two young daughters. On 17 October 1861, at age twenty-nine, John married twenty-four-year-old Annie Frances Price.

The Civil War was then raging, but, probably because of his age and family status, John Bertholf did not volunteer for military service. The war dragged on, however, and the Union needed more troops. By 1863 the Lincoln administration had approved the organization of black regiments to fight in the war. During February and March of that year, Brig. Gen. Daniel Ullman recruited enough white officers in New York City to lead a brigade of black troops then being organized in Louisiana. John Bertholf was among those officers.

In May 1863 Bertholf accompanied Ullman to Louisiana. Because of his business background, John was commissioned a first lieutenant and made the adjutant of Company K of the 7th Infantry Regiment, Corps d'Afrique. Ullman's brigade saw combat action during the siege of Port Hudson from 23 May to 8 July 1863. In April 1864 the 7th Infantry Regiment, Corps d'Afrique, was redesignated the 79th U.S. Colored Infantry Regiment. In August the 79th was transferred to Morganza, Louisiana, for garrison duty. The regiment remained there until October 1864, when the 79th was broken up and its enlisted men sent to replenish other regiments. Many of the regiment's white officers, including John Bertholf, were mustered out of the service.[1]

John Bertholf returned to his wife and two daughters in New York City, arriving there in time to celebrate their third wedding anniversary and the birth of their first child, Edward Oscar, born 23 October 1864. John, now the proud father of a son, returned to his accounting position. Less than two years later, on 7 April 1866, Annie gave birth to their second son, Ellsworth Price, who was named for a relative on his mother's side of the family. John and Annie had no way of knowing that their baby boy would grow up to be a national hero fêted by the president and Congress of the United States.

Young Ellsworth spent the first few years of his life in New York City. When he was four, a baby brother, John Winthrop, joined the family on 2 April 1870. Shortly after this birth the family moved across the Hudson River from New York City into the bustling New Jersey village of Hackensack. By this time Ellsworth had received the nickname "Todd," by which he would be known throughout his childhood. It was probably much easier for his younger sibling to pronounce than "Ellsworth."

The Bertholfs' new hometown, located on the Hackensack River, had long been the county seat of Bergen County, New Jersey. Organized as New Barbadoes in 1676 by Dutch settlers, Hackensack was largely a village of pleasant homes with the beginnings of a few industrial and manufacturing activities. For the past one hundred years it had been the center of trade for the area within fifty to seventy-five miles to the north-west. From the commanding heights on its western border young Todd Bertholf could see the river winding through the valley below, with the range of the Palisades beyond and New York City twelve miles away in the distance. There was a great deal of boat traffic on the Hackensack River, especially in the fall and spring, when farm and industrial products were transported by water to Newark and New York. It would later be said of young Todd that "as a boy in New Jersey he found the broad Hackensack River an expanse of unlimited wonders, and knowing that it flowed down to join the Raritan and then through Newark Bay to the sea, he loved it because it typified his own young ambitions—to finally reach the ocean."[2] Bertholf himself would later say that he believed that some men were born to the life of a soldier or sailor and that "the spirit which first takes a boy to sea, follows him straight through life."[3]

The Bertholf family continued to increase during Todd's childhood. From 1872 to 1884 seven more siblings were born: three sisters and four brothers. The Bertholf home, an old colonial house in a residential section of the village near the downtown area, on Huyler Street between Essex and Kansas, was undoubtedly a beehive of activity. To support his growing family John Bertholf set up shop as an accountant and auctioneer near the Bergen County Courthouse at the center of the village. His office, on Main Street between Passaic and Essex Streets, was only a couple of blocks from his home.[4]

Until the age of six or so, Todd, like all young boys of his time, was enmeshed in a domestic world dominated by women: his two older half-sisters and his mother. His half-sisters were more than ten years older than he was and more like adults to him than siblings. Chances to stray from their watchful eyes were probably rare. It was a time when mothers kept an especially close eye on their younger children in accordance with the widely held belief that the basis for good character was laid during this phase of a boy's life.

When he reached the age of six, young Todd entered another world as well—in reality a subculture, a boy culture. For the remainder of his childhood he shuttled constantly between the female-dominated world of his home and the world of his boyhood friends. His experiences with other boys helped prepare him in many ways for adulthood. The boys went sledding and skating in the winter, and hiking, swimming, and exploring during the summer. Boy culture was surprisingly free of adult intervention, and his interactions with his playmates gave him his first exhilarating taste of independence and made a lasting imprint on his character.[5]

Anthony Rotundo, who has described the importance of the boy culture in the lives of boys in late nineteenth-century America, notes that it embraced two sorts of values: the traits and behaviors boys openly respected in one another and the implicit values embedded in the culture's structure. Both sets of values became permanent parts of a boy's character. This was undoubtedly true for young Todd. Rotundo argues that while boys valued loyalty and physical prowess, the trait they consciously held in highest esteem was courage.[6]

There are no records of Bertholf's youth, but his later conduct at the Naval Academy and the Revenue-Cutter Service School of Instruction indicates that he was a boy drawn to rule breaking by the possibility of a clash with authority. Boys often dared each other to perform dangerous acts. Since confrontations with adults held inherent danger, they were considered a way to prove one's courage. Pranks served as skirmishes in the guerrilla warfare that boys waged against adults.[7] Such pranks, much like Bertholf's later pranks as a cadet, were seen as mischief, not wickedness. Boys, and their parents too, for the most part, considered them wholesome fun.

As soon as he was old enough, Todd began school. Annie, like other middle-class mothers of the era, more than likely hoped that school would "civilize" her son, who must sometimes have seemed like a young savage. Todd, for his part, probably looked forward to school as a place free of the constant restrictions of his home. School gave him the opportunity to interact with other boys his age in a structured environment. The boy culture and school culture were constantly at odds. It was not uncommon for nineteenth-century boys to take pleasure in flouting their teacher's authority at school.

Little is known of Bertholf's years in grammar school, though he must have often walked by the town green fronting on Main Street. The green, in the shape of a parallelogram with sides of about 120 feet on Main Street and about 200 feet between Court and Mansion Streets, was shaded by lofty elms and ancient weeping willows. In the center were a tall flagpole, a fountain, and a bandstand. As a boy of eight, Todd probably joined the crowd that gathered on the green to catch a glimpse of Ulysses S. Grant as the president passed through Hackensack on his way to Paterson and the reunion of the Grand Army of the Republic (GAR).[8]

We may also suppose that Todd grew up with a sense of the history of his colonial village. Certainly he learned that the feet of Washington and Lafayette and the patriotic soldiers of the American Revolution had marched across Hackensack's village green. Here, too, the "forefathers of the hamlet" of Revolutionary days saw their courthouse burned to ashes and the town sacked and plundered by British invaders.

Young Todd probably accompanied his family to services at the old Dutch Reformed church that faced one side of the green, but there is no indication that he found any calling there. Most likely, Todd, like most other boys of his age, left Sunday school after age twelve and never returned.

It was the Bertholf family's good fortune that Hackensack was the home of the prestigious Washington Institute, established in 1779. When the time came for Todd to begin his secondary education, he was enrolled in the institute, which was then located in a two-story brick building on the corner of Main and Warren Streets. The institute's building was designed to accommodate 130 students. By 1876, however, when Bertholf entered, more than 260 students were crowded into the old building with nearly 100 more seeking admission. So great was the Washington Institute's reputation that many parents from the surrounding area who had the means sent their children there. The school's students scored the highest marks in proficiency in Bergen County, and the institute was considered one of the leading schools in the state.

In 1877 a meeting of the citizens of the school district considered the steps necessary to build a new and larger schoolhouse. A new site was selected on the northwest corner of Union and Myers Streets, near the center of the population and less than one-fourth of a mile from the courthouse facing the village green. Construction began in the spring of 1878. When it was finished, on 2 December 1878, the school was one of the largest buildings in the village, with four classrooms on each of its four stories, blackboards on all four sides of each classroom, and steam heat warming all the rooms.

Hackensack was very proud of its new school, but even prouder of the school's principal, Nelson Haas. Principal Haas was so well respected that Rutgers College conferred on him the honorary degree of master of arts in 1877. Before the Civil War, Nelson Haas was a teacher in Pennsylvania and Mississippi. During the war Haas served the Union first as a provost marshal in Pennsylvania and then as a first lieutenant of Company B, 9th

Union League Regiment. After the war Haas studied law and opened a law practice in Stockton, California, before returning to the East.[9]

Principal of the Washington Institute since 1871, Haas was also its leading teacher. The course of studies at the school embraced geometry, trigonometry (plane and spherical), and differential and integral calculus in addition to the higher branches in the sciences and the Greek and Latin languages. Haas prepared his students well and ingrained in them a love for their country and its traditions, both the Revolutionary War traditions of the community and the Civil War values of freedom and equality for all. Haas also maintained strict discipline at the school. A contemporary observer noted that "the school-house No. 32 is a most beautiful structure, and is surrounded by lawns without wires or guards, but upon which not a scholar ever encroaches. They know the invisible lines and obey."[10]

Nelson Haas had a profound influence on Todd Bertholf. Many years later, when Hackensack was considering naming its new high school after Haas, Bertholf wrote a letter to the *Hackensack Republican* offering his opinion of his childhood teacher: "As I remember, he was a bit of a disciplinarian . . . but it was good for us, and withal we youngsters liked him, although we stood very much in awe. He certainly understood boys, and knew not only how to teach, but how to manage, his pupils, and few teachers can point to greater success along those lines."[11]

Bertholf was not alone in his esteem for Haas. When Haas died in 1906, the *Hackensack Republican* was unstinting in its praise for the institute's principal.

> His commanding presence, sonorous voice, and athletic arm, combined to work a miracle among the refractory youth. If a boy attempted to manifest a desire to become boss, the new teacher took him in hand with a promptness and vigor that cooled the aspiring ardor and left the hero in a condition of dilapidated defeat and humiliation. Corporal punishment had been abolished, but Nelson Haas forgot this fact: When a pupil persisted in disregard of propriety and manifested a determination to be "smart," the new teacher did not hesitate to display his physical prowess in a successful manner. . . .
>
> As all know, the absorbing purpose of Prof. Haas was to implant in his pupils the element of success in life. His ability to read character and detect the capabilities of the boys and girls under his care was marvelous. He never

made a mistake in the boys he selected to enter the West Point and Annapolis appointment competitions. Every boy who had his approval was a winner. He knew his lads and impressed them with his own force and determination so thoroughly that they absorbed the intelligence and confidence which carried them to the winner's goal.[12]

Todd Bertholf was among those "lads" who gained Professor Haas's approval, but Bertholf later noted that this fact was a "commentary not so much upon the boys as the man who taught these boys."[13]

Todd Bertholf grew up listening to stories of the Civil War told by its veterans—his father and Professor Haas among them. Both men were members of James B. McPherson Post Number 8 of the GAR. The men who fought in the Civil War were set apart by that experience. They had learned, in Oliver Wendell Holmes's words, "that life is a profound and passionate thing."[14] Members of the next generation, Bertholf's generation, yearned for a way in which they too could prove themselves courageous. Teddy Roosevelt expounded this desire and the lifestyle it engendered in a speech entitled "The Strenuous Life" given before the Hamilton Club in Chicago on 10 April 1899. His opening remarks offer insight into the common values of the time.

> In speaking to you, men of the greatest city of the West, men of the State which gave to the country Lincoln and Grant, men who pre-eminently and distinctly embody all that is most American in the American character, I wish to preach, not the doctrine of ignoble ease, but the doctrine of the strenuous life, the life of toil and effort, of labor and strife; to preach that the highest form of success . . . comes, not to the man who desires easy peace, but to the man who does not shrink from danger, from hardship, or from bitter toil, and who out of these winds the splendid ultimate triumph.[15]

The urbanization and industrialization that occurred at the end of the nineteenth century, with the sedentary and routine work environments they created, were thought to undermine men's dignity and independence. It was a time when men searched for ways to reassure themselves of their masculinity. Many of Bertholf's generation preferred to be tested by physical struggle rather than looking for success as businessmen. Military service was held in particularly high regard.[16]

In June 1881, in Bertholf's senior year, he and his classmates participated in the county's first competitive examination of scholars. That the
students of the Washington Institute received more first-grade diplomas
than the students in all the rest of the county, and bore a higher standard
of scholarship, was accredited to Prof. Haas's thorough preparation.[17]

Bertholf and his classmates graduated at a joint Bergen County commencement exercise held at the First Reformed Church (the old Dutch
Reformed church on the green) on Friday, 1 July 1881. Parents and
friends filled every seat in the church, including the balcony. Preceded
by their teachers, Bertholf and the other "successful scholars" from the
county's schools marched down the main aisle of the church. It was the
first commencement exercise for the public schools of Bergen County.
With his family undoubtedly proudly looking on, Todd Bertholf received
a "first grade" diploma indicating that he had obtained a grade average
of 75 percent or above.[18]

While Bertholf was in high school, Professor Haas had encouraged
him to consider competing for an appointment to the U.S. Naval Academy at Annapolis, Maryland. The decision to try for a career in the navy
required serious consideration. It was a difficult time for the U.S. Navy,
largely because the nation was concentrating on domestic rather than
foreign affairs. During the almost two decades since the Civil War the
navy had been relegated to a minor role in American life and ranked only
twelfth in size among the world's naval forces. Promotion was by seniority, and the "hump" created by the large number of officers commissioned during the Civil War made promotion so slow that many men who
were lieutenants in 1869 were still lieutenants twelve years later.

This promotion logjam also affected the young men at the Naval
Academy. Before the Civil War, students at the academy were appointed
midshipmen while they were still in school and commissioned ensigns
shortly after graduation. After the war, academy students were called "naval
cadets" and became midshipmen only on graduation. Many graduates of
the academy were obliged to wait a decade or more before receiving their
commissions as ensigns.[19] These poor career prospects were certainly
enough to make an ambitious young man pause and reflect. Nevertheless, with Professor Haas's encouragement, young Bertholf decided to
enter the competitive examination for appointment to the Naval Academy at Annapolis when it was announced by Congressman John Hill of
the Fifth Congressional District of New Jersey. At sixteen, Bertholf stood

at the midpoint of the age range of fourteen to eighteen years established for admission to the academy.

The examination was held in Paterson on 1 June.[20] Each of the mathematical questions was worth the same number of points, notwithstanding the fact that some were much harder than others. The time allotted to work out the answers to the questions was designed to be short of the time necessary to do them all, so even the best students were expected to have some uncompleted problems when time was called. Bertholf not only solved all eight of the mathematical problems (two had been stricken out by the examiners) but also did his work in thirty-five minutes less than the allotted time of two hours.[21]

Sixteen-year-old Bertholf finished sixteen points ahead of his closest competitor and won the appointment over the other applicants from the Fifth District, which comprised not only his home county of Bergen but also Morris and Passaic Counties. He subsequently was appointed a naval cadet by Congressman John Hill and directed to report to the Naval Academy in September. In the fall of 1882 he left his hometown of four thousand people and journeyed south to Maryland to begin his military career.

~❧ 2 ❧~

THE CADET YEARS

S ixteen-year-old Ellsworth Bertholf was among the younger nominees who walked through the main gate at the Naval Academy in Annapolis, Maryland, on 22 September 1882. The cadets came from all parts of the country and from homes of varying degrees of wealth, but all were determined to become naval officers. Ellsworth and his future classmates spent their first few days at the academy undergoing a final battery of physical and academic examinations. After passing all the tests, young Bertholf took the oath of allegiance with his fellow members of the academy's class of 1886 on 28 September and became a naval cadet.

On entering the academy, Bertholf left behind the female-dominated world of his home and entered a totally male environment dominated by older adolescents and young men only nominally under the supervision of navy officers. The new world was a boys' world of pranks, competition, rebellion, and humor. Like all of the boys, Bertholf brimmed with an energy that threatened continually to overflow the academy's rigid discipline.

The academy, located on the northeast edge of Annapolis on a point of land jutting out into the Severn River, had two distinct four-year courses of study, one for engineers and another for line officers. Students who chose to follow the former course would become engineering

officers on navy ships, responsible for the operation, care, and maintenance of all propulsion and auxiliary machinery, and for controlling all
damage to the ship. Line officers are, by definition, naval officers eligible for command at sea. Bertholf pursued the line officer track. He and
the other cadets resided in New Quarters, a dormitory built in 1869 that
also contained the mess hall.

The cadets received regular visual reminders of the courage, sacrifice,
and glorious deeds of U.S. Navy officers. Every time he entered or
departed New Quarters, Bertholf passed by the ornately carved Tripoli
Monument built in memory of the six navy officers who fell in the attack
on Tripoli in 1804. As Bertholf marched to classes he passed the much
simpler Mexican Monument erected in memory of four midshipmen
who sacrificed their lives in the Mexican War. This oldest monument on
the academy grounds, erected in 1848, consisted of a marble shaft supported by a rectangular base and four upright cannons. Bertholf also
passed the Herndon Monument, a massive shaft of Quincy granite erected in 1859 to commemorate Comdr. William Louis Herndon, who
went down with the mail steamer *Central America* in a storm off Cape
Hatteras in September 1867. After making every possible effort to save
the ship, Herndon left the quarterdeck long enough to don his full-dress
uniform, in which he returned to his post to meet a seaman's death. The
monuments were a constant reminder to Bertholf and his fellow cadets
of the sacrifice often required of navy officers and the glory that those
who had gone before them had brought to the academy. The monuments
would inspire young Bertholf and many others who saw them to face
similar difficulties with courage and determination.

The academic year of 1882–83, Bertholf's first year at the academy, was
the most troubled that the academy had ever experienced. In November
1881 the new superintendent, Capt. Francis M. Ramsay, began institut-
ing sweeping changes. The curriculum was revised, and professional
subjects were postponed until cadets' first-class (final) year. Room
assignments in New Quarters were changed as well. Rather than being
assigned housing on the basis of class year, as before, cadets were now
assigned according to the company within the cadet battalion to which
they belonged, which included cadets of all four classes. The first-class
cadet officers were made responsible for maintaining good order in the
dormitories. Upperclassmen viewed the change in the system of quartering

as an assault on their time-honored class privileges. The only aspect of academy life that seemed untouched by Ramsay's reforms was the traditional style of instruction. Courses continued to be conducted almost exclusively by the recitation method. On entering the classroom, cadets were invited to "draw slips" on which the instructor had written various problems or questions, and to "man the boards" to work out the problems.

The navy's unmanageable surplus of officers was affecting the cadets at the academy as well. By the beginning of the 1880s there was one officer for every four enlisted men, and it was taking Annapolis graduates as long as eight years after graduation to make ensign. In 1881 Adm. David Porter recommended three solutions to eliminate the logjam that directly affected the Naval Academy: reduce the number of cadets entering the Naval Academy, increase the standards of admission, and graduate and commission only twenty officers each year.[1]

When the Department of the Navy failed to act on Porter's advice, Congress stepped in. The month before Bertholf had arrived at Annapolis Congress passed the Personnel Act of 5 August 1882, which stipulated that no graduate of the Naval Academy could be appointed an officer unless there were two vacancies on the lineal list. Furthermore, appointments were to be made on the basis of class standing. The act also attempted to ease the friction that existed between line officers and engineers; the latter took a different course of instruction and had better promotion opportunities. Hoping to nip their differences in the bud, the act abolished the titles of "cadet-midshipman" and "cadet-engineer," and substituted the all-embracing "naval cadet," which pleased no one.[2]

Of the sixty-three graduates of the class of 1881, who had already joined the fleet for their two-year probationary period, only twenty-three were retained in the navy under the new law. Twenty-one of the thirty-seven graduates of the class of 1882 either were discharged or resigned under the shadow of the act. To compound the injury, Congress did not award them the previously agreed upon severance pay of a year's salary; the legislators concluded that a free education was remuneration enough.[3]

The act undoubtedly had a negative impact on morale and discipline at the Naval Academy. The cadets knew that under the new law less than one-third of the graduates of any class would have a chance of getting into the navy. Six years of their lives spent in preparation and anticipation of a career in military service would go for naught. Military historian Merrill Bartlett notes that "disorderly conduct, an increased tendency to ignore rules and regulations, and a disinclination to apply themselves to their studies punctuated the behavior of the naval cadets for years" after the act of 5 August 1882 was passed.[4]

It is impossible to say whether the new regulations or his own inclinations were responsible for Bertholf's behavior at the academy. Throughout his time as a naval cadet, Bertholf was always near the top of his class in both marks and demerits. His name was a frequent entry in the conduct book. Judging by the pages of this large book, the sixteen-year-old naval cadet epitomized late Victorian boyhood with its values of bold actions, courage, and daring. His sins were usually minor: throwing chalk in class, leaving the light on in his room after "lights out," not making his bed, and being late to morning formations. From time to time he was caught playing cards or visiting in another cadet's room when he was supposed to be studying in his own.[5]

The academic schedule kept Bertholf and his classmates busy six days a week. On Sundays they marched to church services at the academy chapel unless they elected to go to a church of their own faith in Annapolis. Bertholf had received permission to do the latter early that first fall, choosing to worship at a local Reformed church rather than at the Episcopal services at the academy. It also provided an opportunity for him to break free from the strict discipline of the academy grounds each Sunday morning.

Infantry drill on the parade ground was a regular part of the daily routine. It was held near the old mulberry tree, the foremost landmark of the academy at the time. During drills, cadets learned the manual of arms and different marching commands as well as the intense discipline and focus that infantry drill requires. Young Bertholf was placed on report repeatedly for talking in ranks or being disorderly in ranks during drill. In the spring of his first year he was assigned extra drill periods as an incentive to improve his demeanor and performance.

But a cadet's life was not just academic and military training. Adm. David Porter, who had served as superintendent of the academy from 1865 to 1869, had developed the social life at the academy to such an extent that the institution was often called "Porter's Dancing Academy" by the wits of the day. Regular balls were held in the interior of old Fort Severn, which at the time served as the academy's gymnasium. Early in January the first class gave a formal ball, which was followed six weeks later by the second

class's dress hop. These were grand affairs often attended by cabinet officers, members of Congress, and foreign dignitaries.[6]

The rage for competitive athletics had not yet reached the Naval
Academy or other college campuses in the 1880s. Almost the only competitive outlet for Bertholf and his fellow naval cadets was rowing. Lack-
ing other activities to draw off their excess energy, many of the cadets,
including Bertholf, channeled their aggression and high spirits into
rebellion against the academy's strict discipline.

Early football had been introduced at the academy in 1857, but the
cadets soon lost interest in it. The evolution of early football away from
the old rugby rules into an entirely new game in the late nineteenth century reawakened the cadets' interest. In Bertholf's first few months at
Annapolis, Cadet Vaulx Carter of the class of 1884 provided the impetus
for the formation of the Navy team. On 30 November 1882, Thanksgiv-
ing Day, Bertholf and his fellow cadets got to witness the academy's football team play its first game against an outside opponent. Buoyed by the
cadets' enthusiastic cheers, Navy defeated the Johns Hopkins University
team. In 1885 the single-game season was expanded to three games, and
in 1886 to six.[7] The rivalry between the Naval Academy and the Military
Academy was not initiated until four years later, in November 1890.

Shortly after watching that first football game Bertholf was placed in
conduct class 4 (the lowest class) for having an "excess" of demerits that
month.[8] Only a week later, on the afternoon of 6 December, Bertholf was
caught dumping water from an upper-corridor window on cooks and
"truckmen" below. For this prank he was awarded seven demerits. At the
end of January his misconduct resulted in the loss of all privileges and
assignment to the *Santee* for one month. The *Santee* was an old frigate
that served as a brig, and assignment there was supposed to be punishment reserved for the most serious cadet offenders, but for most naval
cadets at the time it had become a rite of passage. Even while assigned
to the *Santee* Cadet Bertholf continued to be a risk taker. He was placed
on report for being absent from the ship without permission for almost
an hour. He was also caught with tobacco in his possession and caught
attempting to supply a cadet in solitary confinement with tobacco and a
novel.[9] The latter infraction might be charitably interpreted as empathy
for one whose conduct had earned this severest of punishments.

The cadets' resentment over the changes instituted by Captain Ramsay and the devastating effects of the Personnel Act of 5 August 1882

boiled over in January 1883. First-class Cadet Petty Officer Charles E. Woodruff posted the answers to a mathematics examination he had just completed inside the door of a hall closet for the benefit of his slower classmates. When he learned about it, Captain Ramsay deprived Cadet Woodruff of his rank. The cadets were informed of the action during the customary reading aloud of orders at dinner formation. As Woodruff's division marched out of the mess hall after the meal, the student body, led by Cadet Lt. George W. Street, gave him a cheer. Street, too, lost his stripes. Not a man to tolerate insubordination, Captain Ramsay transferred the entire first class to the *Santee* and imposed severe restrictions on the other classes. Virtually all of the first-class cadet officers tendered their resignations as a result. The reaction of the cadet battalion was not far removed from mutiny. In formation, the cadets expressed their opinion of orders with groans, hisses, laughter, and impertinent cheers.[10]

On 30 January, after completing his assignment on the *Santee*, Bertholf was among those charged with "mutinous conduct" for cheering a first-class cadet in defiance of the superintendent's order.[11] Early in February he was caught again attempting to communicate with and supply a novel to his classmate, Cadet John P. Knettles, while Knettles was in solitary confinement.

Bertholf's behavior did not improve during the second term. One of his favorite ways to annoy upperclassmen was to scrape his shoes in ranks while marching to class, even after being ordered to stop. On another occasion he "skylarked" (turned his head to look around him rather than looking only at the boat's coxswain) during a boat drill on the Severn River, again after being ordered to stop. By late spring his continual tardiness to morning formations had resulted in orders that he be awakened at 5:00 A.M. and report to the officer in charge at 6:00 each morning for a week. He failed to report on time one morning and the punishment was extended for two more weeks.

The frustration of the naval cadets reached its climax at the graduation ceremony. Cadets, faculty, staff, distinguished guests, and parents assembled in the chapel for the presentation of diplomas on the morning of 9 June 1883. The speaker, Representative R. T. Mills of Texas, emphasized the necessity for cheerful obedience to orders. Following the congressman's address, Captain Ramsay arose to begin presenting the diplomas. He leaned against the podium and said something, although only a few people heard him. As Cadet Dana S. Greene Jr., the honor man, stepped forward to be the first to receive his diploma, a number of cadets broke into cheers, the usual course on commencement day when a favorite steps up to receive his diploma. The infuriated Captain Ramsay ordered all the cadets to rise and the ones who had applauded to step forward. Twenty cadets stepped forward and were ordered confined to the *Santee.* The diplomas were then handed to the remaining graduates in absolute silence.

Only later did the cadets learn that the first words Captain Ramsay had spoken, which almost no one had heard, were that there would be no applause for individual cadets. Just before the ceremony Captain Ramsay had learned that the cadets planned to humiliate one of the cadet officers who had refused to resign with the others by loudly applauding his classmates when their diplomas were presented but leaving him to receive his in silence. It was to avert this ignominy that Ramsay forbade the cadets to applaud. When some officers and cadets explained the situation to Captain Ramsay, he relented and ordered the release of all those who had been confined on the *Santee.* Within an hour all the cadets were once more on liberty off the academy grounds.[12]

Despite the painful and gloomy graduation ceremony, Bertholf and his classmates rejoiced in the fact that they were now third classmen and would no longer be the lowest of the underclassmen. Bertholf and a portion of his class were ordered to report to the oldest ship in the U.S. Navy, the *Constellation,* for the annual summer practice cruise. The *Constellation,* a 164-foot frigate launched on 7 September 1797, had served with distinction in the undeclared naval war with France as a part of the newly reborn U.S. Navy. It had participated in the blockade of Tripoli in May 1802 and in the War of 1812. During the Civil War the *Constellation* sailed the Mediterranean guarding Union merchant ships against attack by Confederate cruisers and privateers. It was fitting that this ship, with its glorious history, had been selected to serve as the Naval Academy's primary training ship.

Bertholf and the other cadets embarked on 11 June. The quarters aboard the *Constellation* were cramped; the cadets slept in hammocks and lived like common sailors. After leaving Annapolis on 16 June, the ship with its young crew sailed down the Chesapeake Bay and reached the Atlantic Ocean on 25 June. From there the *Constellation* turned north toward New England.

As one of the twenty-three third-class cadets aboard the *Constellation* young Bertholf was assigned watches and stations with the crew. He performed the duties of petty officers and seaman, but he was not required to clean the ship. While on the practice cruise Bertholf, the other third-class men, and the newly reported fourth classmen learned a wide variety of practical seamanship skills. Bertholf had arrived at the academy too late to make his first cruise as a fourth classman.

Cadet Bertholf's conduct aboard the *Constellation* continued to earn him demerits. Less than two weeks after the practice cruise began he was found asleep under a boom cover when he was supposed to be on watch. He was assigned two extra lookout watches as punishment. Because of an excessive number of demerits Bertholf was denied liberty when the *Constellation* arrived at Portsmouth, New Hampshire, on 16 July. In the weeks that followed the ship's departure from Portsmouth on 31 July, Bertholf was caught reading on the gun deck when he was supposed to be on watch and received another two lookout watches. For "shirking church" he was awarded three extra lookout watches.[13] Bertholf's involvement in hazing during the practice cruise proved to be the costliest misconduct of all.

Hazing, traditionally carried out by third classmen against fourth classmen, had been introduced at the academy during the Civil War. By the early 1870s hazing practices ranged from mildly absurd to really brutal. In June 1874 Congress, in response to parental complaints, had adopted a bill that became known as the "Hazing Law" forbidding hazing at the Naval Academy. Under the Hazing Law any cadet accused of hazing would be court-martialed and dismissed from the academy if found guilty. The law further provided that any cadet dismissed for hazing would be forever ineligible for reappointment to the academy. Unfortunately, as Jack Sweetman notes of the law in his history of the academy, "aside from abbreviating some of their careers, its principal impact on the cadets was to increase the spice of indulging in a practice whose imprudence was already among its chief attractions. As Congress after Congress and superintendent after superintendent discovered to their annoyance and chagrin, that act did not inhibit hazing."[14]

Several hazing incidents were being investigated onboard the *Constellation* as it sailed back to Annapolis in the summer of 1883. Some of them had occurred in June while the ship was sailing to Portsmouth, and others in July while it was anchored in Portsmouth harbor. On 25 August, while the ship was sailing up the Chesapeake Bay, Cadet Bertholf and several of his classmates were formally charged with hazing. When the *Constellation* arrived back at Annapolis on 28 August, all the naval cadets were graded for their performance on the cruise. Bertholf received a 3.18 for his general duties, but only a 2.90 for his conduct.

On 31 August Captain Ramsay convened a court-martial to try the third-class cadets accused of violating the Hazing Law. The court-martial made national news and received daily coverage in the *New York Times* and other large newspapers. The first cadet tried was Benjamin Trapnell, who had the most numerous and serious hazing charges against him. Trapnell's alleged acts included making some fourth-class cadets stand on their heads while wearing only nightshirts, making another sit cross-legged in his hammock while he swung the hammock until the underclassman was thrown to the deck, and making another lie motionless in a tank in the washroom for ten minutes. The court convicted Trapnell.

That same day the court also tried Cadets E. T. Witherspoon and D. M. Young. Both were acquitted of all charges when witnesses testified either that the two young men were not present during the hazing incidents or that if they were present, they did not annoy or harass any fourth classmen. In commenting on the first day of the court-martial the *New York Times* noted that "the Fourth Class men are very unwilling witnesses, and the most searching questions were asked them without avail. Whenever they can acquit their persecutors, the Third Class men, they do so. The court evidently understands this and puts questions to cover every phase of the matter."[15]

On the afternoon of 3 September Cadet Bertholf was placed on trial to face three charges: first, along with other cadets, that he made Cadet T. S. Jewett stand on his head while the *Constellation* was cruising Chesapeake Bay the previous June; second, that he required Cadets T. M. O'Halloran, H. C. Rodgers, and G. W. Galloway to turn out of their hammocks after 9:00 P.M. and stand on their hands while the ship was at Portsmouth, New Hampshire; and third, that he required five other fourth-class cadets to stand on their heads on the berth deck, thereby causing them to "make indecent exposures of their persons." While some of the accused cadets had chosen to be represented by legal counsel, Bertholf defended himself. He pleaded not guilty to all the charges.

Naval Cadet T. S. Jewett, the first witness for the prosecution, testified that he had not been ordered to stand on his head by Bertholf. When the prosecutor asked him if he had ever stood on his head on the berth deck, and if so, by whose order, Jewett answered that it was by the order of Frederick N. Kress. Bertholf objected to this second question on the ground that it had no bearing on his case, but his objection was overruled. Jewett went on to testify that Bertholf had not even been present when Kress had ordered him to stand on his head. Bertholf had no questions.

The prosecution then moved to the second specification and called Naval Cadet T. M. O'Halloran to the witness stand. Cadet O'Halloran testified that both Trapnell and Bertholf had stood by his hammock, but he could not say which one had ordered him to turn out. O'Halloran did state that Bertholf was present throughout the hazing and that there was no difference between the actions of Cadet Trapnell and Cadet Bertholf.

The following day, 4 September, Bertholf's trial reconvened. Naval Cadet H. C. Rodgers testified that the accused required him, on or about 30 July, to turn out of his hammock and stand on his head. Cadet G. W. Galloway testified that while Bertholf was present, he never required him to turn out of his hammock or stand on his head. Cadet E. Durell testified that he did not think that Bertholf had made him stand on his head for the purpose of exposing himself, but rather as a matter of fun. Cadet F. Moore gave similar testimony. Cadets Guthrie and Peckham testified that they were required to stand on their heads, but could not say who ordered them or even that Bertholf was present. Cadet G. W. Fitzgerald, the ninth and final witness, stated that he had been ordered to stand on his head by Cadet Trapnell. Bertholf's hometown newspaper, the *Hackensack Republican,* which was following the trial closely, concluded that serious evidence had been presented against "our cadet."[16]

The court-martial found Bertholf not guilty of the first specification but guilty of the second specification and also of the third, except as to the indecent exposure of the person of Naval Cadet F. G. Moore. In accordance with the act of 23 June 1874, the court went on to recommend that Bertholf be dismissed from the academy.[17] Captain Ramsay, the superintendent, approved the court's recommendation. Bertholf was formally dismissed effective 12 September; his official dismissal notice was delivered to him the following day.[18] On the very next day, 14 September, Bertholf, now a dismissed naval cadet, testified in behalf of his fellow accused classmate, Cadet Edwin Van Deusen Johnson, stating that he was present when the hazing took place and knew that Johnson was not there.[19] Cadet Johnson was acquitted; several others were not.

The *Hackensack Republican* expressed sincere regret for "the fate that has overtaken 'Todd,' who is a bright boy, and stood high in his class. But he who dances must pay the piper. The Government has determined to drive from its schools the practice of hazing, and there is no likelihood that its decision in these cases will be reversed."[20]

In the end, seven naval cadets were dismissed for hazing. Two others were made to repeat their third-class year. Bertholf, now in some disgrace in his hometown, moved to New York City and got a job as a clerk. He hired a law firm to appeal for his pardon. On 3 December the secretary of navy denied the appeal and advised Bertholf that the only way he could be reinstated would be by special legislation of Congress.[21]

Even though he was expelled from the Naval Academy, Bertholf was always proud of his attendance there. When the time came for him to list the key facts of his life for his entry in *Who's Who in America,* he included his membership in the Naval Academy class of 1886. In later years, while he was living in Washington, D.C., Bertholf would attend Naval Academy Graduates Association dinners as a member of the class of 1886.[22]

Though all hope of reinstatement to the Naval Academy was now gone, Ellsworth Bertholf did not cease striving to become a military officer. He had been taught not to shrink from difficulties but to overcome them. He decided to compete for a congressional appointment to the U.S. Military Academy at West Point for the class entering in 1884. He was successful in that competition, but before the appointment could be confirmed, an unsuccessful competitor objected that Bertholf had not lived in the city long enough to be a legal resident, and was thus not entitled to the appointment. The appointment was withdrawn.[23]

Thus thwarted in his attempts to become an officer in either the navy or the army, Bertholf returned to Hackensack to live with his parents and siblings, still determined to have a career in the military. His thirst for adventure and "manly" activities would allow no other course. When he saw an announcement from the Revenue-Cutter Service dated 29 June 1885 stating that not enough applicants had qualified in the annual exam for admission to the service's School of Instruction and informing the public that a second exam would be held at the end of August in Washington, D.C., Bertholf decided to compete for an appointment.[24]

Established in 1790 as a fleet of ten armed revenue cutters to prevent smuggling and ensure the payment of tariff revenues—one of the chief sources of income for the federal government in the eighteenth and nineteenth centuries—the Revenue-Cutter Service was well known to those who lived in American maritime cities. Besides preventing smuggling, the service also protected American merchant vessels and their crews from pirates. The Revenue-Cutter Service was both an auxiliary navy and a servant that met America's civilian maritime needs.

Because its primary mission was to collect tariff duties, the Revenue-Cutter Service was part of the Treasury Department. When the Quasi-War with France broke out in 1798, the vessels in the Revenue-Cutter Service were transferred to the new U.S. Navy as an emergency measure, setting a precedent that was confirmed a year later by an act of Congress. At the end of the Quasi-War the cutters were returned to the Treasury Department, but the precedent set in 1798 placed them in service with the U.S. Navy during subsequent hostilities as well: the War of 1812, the war against piracy in the Caribbean, the Seminole War, the Mexican War, and the Civil War. The Revenue-Cutter Service was organized in military fashion with officers who were commissioned by the president, noncommissioned officers, gunners, and mariners. In the eyes of the general public, it was, if not an armed service, at least an auxiliary military service.

The Revenue-Cutter Service was considerably smaller than the navy, and so was its School of Instruction. One of the factors that made it attractive to Bertholf and many other young men was that unlike Annapolis and West Point, the Revenue-Cutter Service imposed no geographic quotas or political restrictions on its applicants. This meant that appointments were not influenced by political considerations or favoritism, but were made strictly on the basis of merit. Any individual who met the requirement of physical soundness could compete in the annual examinations to fill vacancies. Also, Bertholf's timing was fortuitous. Had he applied after 1905, his dismissal from the Naval Academy for hazing would have rendered him ineligible.[25] Bertholf traveled to Washington in August to compete in the eight-hour examination.[26] He received the fourth-highest score of the fourteen young men who passed the exam, with an average of 83.21 out of 100 points. Candidate Bertholf was appointed a cadet on 4 September 1885.[27]

A few weeks later Bertholf traveled to New Bedford, Massachusetts, the home of the School of Instruction. Once one of New England's major seaports, New Bedford had known great prosperity in the whaling

days, but the falling demand for whale oil and concomitant decline in
the whaling fleet had reduced it to a quieter, but still respectable, existence as a maritime city. Unlike the Naval Academy, which had a multi-
acre campus with numerous buildings in Annapolis, the Revenue-Cutter
School of Instruction was a floating campus entirely contained aboard
a specially constructed school ship, the USRC *Salmon P. Chase*. The
Chase, completed in Philadelphia on 6 August 1787, was a 115-foot,
three-masted bark homeported in New Bedford. Designed by Capt. J. H.
Merryman of the Revenue-Cutter Service and named for Abraham Lincoln's secretary of the treasury, the *Chase* was the last sailing vessel built
for the Revenue-Cutter Service. The *Chase* was much admired for its
sharp lines and speed. In addition to the cadets it carried a complement
of four officers and twenty-eight enlisted men.[28]

The *Chase* was moored at the north end of Fish Island in the middle
of New Bedford harbor, just off New Bedford's main business district.
Although a railroad drawbridge connected the island to the city, the
anchorage was an isolated spot. Not only was the school entirely aboard
this vessel, it was also only a two-year course of instruction, at the completion of which graduates could take the examination for promotion to
third lieutenant.

Bertholf, now nineteen years of age, and seven other newly appointed
cadets in the class of 1887 boarded the *Chase* on 14 September and
reported to Capt. Leonard G. Shepard, commanding officer of the *Chase*
and superintendent of the School of Instruction. They were sworn in as
cadets and officially entered the Revenue-Cutter Service.

The *Chase* would be Bertholf's home and classroom for the next two
years. The steerage, the forward part of the ship where the cadets lived,
contained six staterooms with two berths each, a washstand, and lockers
sufficient for clothing.[29] As at Annapolis, the curriculum included French,
and in addition to instruction in the naval arts the cadets were taught
constitutional and revenue law. The officers assigned to the *Chase* taught
the latter course as well as the seamanship and navigation courses. As a
cadet, Bertholf received nine hundred dollars a year (three-fourths the
salary of a third lieutenant) and one navy ration a day. Shore liberty, to
visit New Bedford, was allowed on Wednesday and Saturday afternoons,
and on Sundays following inspection.[30] Physical fitness was also emphasized. Cadets usually rowed the boats of the *Chase* around New Bedford
harbor for four or five miles before breakfast every morning. During the

winter, when ice closed the harbor, the cadets performed calisthenics each morning from 6:00 to 7:30.[31]

While there is no known conduct record for the cadets during this period, it is probable that Bertholf's behavior at the School of Instruction was not much different from his behavior at the Naval Academy. Although now nineteen years of age, Bertholf was still a rebel. The *Chase*'s log does indicate that Bertholf and four other cadets had their liberty stopped for two weeks for neglecting to attend church on 11 April as required by regulations.[32]

Cadet Bertholf received his primary professional training during the annual summer practice cruise of the *Chase*. On 12 June the *Chase* sailed out of New Bedford harbor, passed through Rhode Island Sound, and headed east toward Spain upon reaching the Atlantic Ocean. Unlike most of his classmates, Bertholf already had experience at sea, having sailed aboard the USS *Constellation* two years earlier. As an underclassman on the *Chase* he did many of the same things he had done as a third classman on the *Constellation*. Much of the training was mere review for him, and he naturally excelled. During periods of calm weather the cadets practiced raising shears; stepping masts; reefing, furling, and shifting sails; and sending yards up and down. Less than a month later, on 8 July, the *Chase* anchored off La Coruña, Spain. Located on Cape Finisterre in northwest Spain, La Coruña was one of Spain's major Atlantic seaports. Two weeks later the *Chase* sailed to São Miguel, the largest island in the Azores, anchoring off the city of Ponta Delgada on 26 July. Following a brief port visit the *Chase* sailed back to the United States. By 23 August the School of Instruction was in the sheltered waters of Gardiner's Bay on the eastern end of Long Island carrying out nautical evolutions.[33] On 10 September the *Chase* returned to New Bedford, where a new class of cadets reported aboard and the upper classmen were detached to prepare for the examination for third lieutenant. As a first classman (second-year cadet), Bertholf's courses included four weeks of steamship engineering and fourteen weeks of law.[34]

Capt. Daniel B. Hodgsdon relieved Captain Shepard as superintendent of the School of Instruction and commanding officer of the *Chase* on 9 April. From Captain Hodgsdon's correspondence we learn that Bertholf was still taking risks and challenging authority during his second year. In May, shortly after becoming superintendent, Captain Hodgsdon wrote to the assistant secretary of the treasury reporting that, pending guidance from the department, he had stopped liberty for four cadets, among them Cadet Bertholf, for "disobedience of orders and violation of regulations." The assistant secretary, I. H. Maynard, responded that since Cadets Bertholf and Wilcox had previously received approval for leave, they would have to be released from the restriction. The letter to Captain Hodgsdon also stated: "You will, however, inform them that a repetition of the offenses will cause them to be considered as undesirable persons to be commissioned officers in the service."[35] Captain Hodgsdon reluctantly allowed the two cadets to go on their previously approved leave, but not before warning them about their unacceptable conduct and its possible consequences.

Bertholf and Wilcox returned from their leaves and with their classmates sailed out of New Bedford harbor on 3 June 1887 for their upperclass practice cruise. That summer the *Chase* sailed to Lisbon, Portugal. Even while sailing across the Atlantic the cadets aboard the *Chase* adhered to a regular military routine. Every Sunday morning, for example, just as when the *Chase* was in New Bedford, the cadets and officers stood at attention in dress uniform on the weather side of the vessel for inspection. As an upperclassman Bertholf learned the duties and responsibilities of a deck officer. Members of his class took turns as "gentleman of the watch" (officer of the deck) on the quarterdeck and "officer of the forecastle" forward. The forecastle watch, on the part of the upper deck of a ship forward of the foremast, was very important on sailing ships because the sails often prevented the officer of the deck from seeing what was in front of the vessel. The forecastle was also the place where the cadets and crew of the *Chase* lived. As a cadet officer under the general supervision of the commissioned officer of the deck, Bertholf handled sails, anticipated squalls, met emergencies, and was considered responsible for the ship. The upperclassmen also practiced celestial navigation, using a sextant to measure the angles of elevation of particular stars above the horizon at a precise time in order to determine the ship's position.

After a month at sea, on the 111th anniversary of America's independence, the *Chase* arrived at Lisbon, then departed two weeks later for the Azores. This year the ship stopped at Faial, one of the central islands in the Azores, anchoring off the city of Horta on 19 July. The school ship departed two days later, sailing back across the Atlantic to the United States. The *Chase* reached Gardiner's Bay on 14 August and after several days of ship's drills and evolutions returned to New Bedford on 2 September.[36]

Bertholf's conduct report for this cruise (the only conduct record in existence for his time at the School of Instruction) indicates little change from his days as a naval cadet, except for the absence of hazing. He was placed on report for not coming promptly on deck when called, for not being prompt in reporting for watches or drills, for lounging on the quarterdeck when on duty, and for wearing inappropriate clothing while on liberty in Lisbon. His twenty-two demerits were the third most infractions, behind Cadet Wilcox with sixty-nine demerits and Cadet Crisp with forty-six. The rest of the cadets onboard had fewer than twelve each. In his report of the practice cruise Captain Hodgsdon recorded the facts regarding Cadets Wilcox, Crisp, Smith, Bertholf, and Robinson along with his opinion that they were unfit to become officers in the Revenue-Cutter Service. His frustration with these conduct problems is evident in his recommendation that the commanding officer be given a more severe means of punishment for offenders than restriction.[37]

His superiors took no action at the time, however, and on 5 September Bertholf and the rest of the class of 1887 were detached from the *Chase* to prepare for their professional examination to become third lieutenants in the Revenue-Cutter Service. Bertholf was officially a graduate of the class of 1887 and always identified himself as such, even though he was not commissioned until 1889. The U.S. Coast Guard Academy Alumni Association mistakenly identifies him as a member of the class of 1889 because that was the year he was commissioned. Because of a shortage of vacancies, the first member of the class of 1887 to be commissioned did not receive his commission until February 1888. The graduates were allowed to return to their homes while awaiting orders to report for the exam, which was held in Washington, D.C., on 18 October 1887.

It was possible to score one hundred points on the exam, with seventy-five fixed as the minimum passing score. Captain Hodgsdon served as the president of the examining board. Of the eight members of his class, Bertholf came in fourth, with an overall score of 79.88. Only the highest-scoring cadet, John B. Hull, was recommended for appointment as a third lieutenant. Four of the cadets were not considered eligible for appointment as third lieutenants because of their low average scores in seamanship. The examining board recommended that they be given six months of probationary service onboard a ship and then be allowed to retake the examination. The board recommended that Cadet Gordon

Wilcox, who scored 75.51 and had a poor conduct record besides, be dismissed from the service.[38]

Cadets Bertholf and Crisp were singled out for special mention. Although both had made satisfactory scores on the exam, their low averages in seamanship—68.39 and 64.29, respectively—and bad conduct on the *Chase* led the board to recommend that they not be considered eligible for promotion to third lieutenant at that time. Instead, the board suggested that they be allowed to continue in the service and placed on probation for about eighteen months, "provided they can show to the satisfaction of the Department that they are amenable to discipline." At the end of the probationary period they would be allowed to retake the examination for promotion to third lieutenant.[39]

The board concluded its report as follows:

> The above recommendations as to Cadets Bertholf, Crisp, and Wilcox are made because the first requisite, indeed necessity, of all organized bodies, in order that they may be effective, is prompt and unquestioning obedience by subordinates of the lawful orders of their superiors. Not only has such obedience not been given by them, but they have persistently violated the rules of the school-ship after having had their attention repeatedly called to them; and Bertholf and Wilcox disregarded a strong warning from the Department.[40]

Disappointed by his probationary status and the delay in his commissioning, Bertholf could at least rejoice at being given another chance to prove himself. He had lost all hope of a career in the navy through his youthful misconduct and now had nearly lost his chance for a career in the Revenue-Cutter Service as well. It was time for Bertholf to reexamine his life and learn the importance of obedience and discipline.

Cadet Bertholf returned to his home to await further orders. On 15 December 1887 he was ordered to report to the USRC *Levi Woodbury*, homeported in Portland, Maine. Launched as the *Mahoning* in 1863 and renamed in June 1873, the *Woodbury* was a 147-foot-long topsail schooner with single-screw propulsion. As a graduate of the School of Instruction, even though still officially a cadet, Bertholf would serve as a deck watch officer. He traveled to Portland and reported aboard for duty on 1 January 1888. Capt. A. B. Fengar would be his commanding officer.

The *Woodbury*'s main cruising area was the New England waters from Cape Ann, Massachusetts, to Portland, Maine.

By 14 January Bertholf had qualified as officer of the day in port and at anchor and would soon qualify as officer of the deck, under way. Qualifying as officer of the deck, under way, was a significant step in Bertholf's early career because it signified the commanding officer's confidence in Bertholf's knowledge, ability, and leadership. The officer of the deck is the officer on watch in charge of the ship and is responsible for the safety of the ship. Every person onboard the ship (except the executive officer), whatever his rank, who is subject to the orders of the commanding officer is subordinate to the officer of the deck. In other words, the officer of the deck is responsible for his ship, has authority commensurate with that responsibility, and is required to exemplify efficiency, dignity, smartness, and zeal in the performance of his duty. There is no counterpart to this position in any other military service and few, if any, in civil life. It is a heavy responsibility, but one that also provides invaluable experience that can be gained only on the bridge of a ship.

During 1888 Bertholf would learn of the commissioning of every one of his classmates except for himself and his fellow probationer Cadet Richard O. Crisp, a sober reminder of the cost of his youthful rebellion. Finally, on 11 May 1889, Cadet Bertholf was allowed to retake the professional examination for third lieutenant in Washington, D.C.[41]

Captain Hodgsdon was still serving as the president of the examining board when it met on 28 May. Cadet Bertholf, now twenty-three years old, did very well on the examination. He received the highest score on the navigation portion, 94.86, and scored 95.56 on the signaling portion; his overall score was 94.554, a close second behind his classmate, Richard Crisp, who received a 94.809. The board recommended both of them for promotion to third lieutenant.[42]

A happy man returned to the *Levi Woodbury*. On 19 June Cadet Bertholf received his temporary commission as a third lieutenant effective 17 June and took the prescribed oath of office.[43] His professional preparation to be a commissioned officer in the service of the United States, begun seven years earlier, had finally come to an end.

3

EARLY CAREER

*A*s a third lieutenant Ellsworth Bertholf could serve as the ordnance (weapons) officer and as a watch officer on any class of vessel in the Revenue-Cutter Service. He continued serving aboard the *Levi Woodbury* in Maine until April 1890. During that time he continued to mature and gained valuable experience as a watch officer.

In April 1890 Bertholf traveled from Portland to Mississippi for duty aboard the USRC *William H. Seward.* One of the Revenue-Cutter Service's older vessels, the 137-foot side-wheel schooner, built in 1864, carried a complement of thirty men. From its homeport in Shieldsborough the *Seward* patrolled the Gulf coast from Mobile, Alabama, to the west end of Lake Pontchartrain, with occasional visits up the mouth of the Mississippi River as far as Jump, above Port Eads and the Passes. Its mission was to prevent smuggling, remove dangerous wrecks from navigable waters, and assist mariners in need.

After just a year and a half, Bertholf transferred to the much newer and larger USRC *Forward* at nearby Mobile. An iron-hulled, twin-screw vessel, the *Forward* carried a topsail schooner/brigantine rig. Bertholf would be one of seven officers aboard the 155-foot cutter, which cruised the Gulf coast from the mouth of the Mississippi to Cedar Key, Florida. While assigned to the *Forward* Bertholf traveled to Washington, D.C., to appear before an examining board and passed both the mental and physical examinations for promotion to the rank of second lieutenant. On 31 October 1892 he assumed the higher rank, which qualified him to serve as navigator on any revenue cutter. As a senior second lieutenant he could be assigned duty as an executive officer at the discretion of the Treasury Department.

Eight months later, in June 1893, the new second lieutenant reported aboard the USRC *Hamilton,* an iron-hulled, single-screw topsail schooner that was being overhauled in a Baltimore shipyard. Only 133 feet in length, the *Hamilton* would be the smallest vessel that Bertholf had yet served on. When all the repairs had been completed, the *Hamilton* sailed from Baltimore on 15 July en route to its homeport of Philadelphia, from which it primarily cruised the Delaware River and Bay. The *Hamilton*'s primary mission was examining vessels entering and leaving the Philadelphia harbor to ensure that they carried no undeclared cargo or contraband. Less than a year after he reported aboard, Bertholf was detached on 5 May 1894 to return to Mobile and the *Forward.*

A year later, still in Mobile, Bertholf learned that his father's health was failing. On 6 May 1895 he sent a telegram to Revenue-Cutter Service Headquarters at the Department of the Treasury requesting ten days' leave because his father was dying. Bertholf's commanding officer aboard the *Forward* had approved the request, and it was granted by the department as well.

Unfortunately, Ellsworth's father died at his home in Hackensack the same day Bertholf sent the telegram. John J. Bertholf, forty-niner and Civil War veteran, was sixty-four years old. Ellsworth did not make it home in time to attend his father's funeral on 9 May, but he was able to be there to comfort his widowed mother and his siblings, three of whom were still under the age of sixteen. His youngest brother, William, born while Ellsworth was a naval cadet at Annapolis, was only eleven years old. Bertholf did not have much time to console his grieving family; within a few weeks he had to leave Hackensack to resume his career.

He did not return immediately to Mobile. While he was in Hackensack Bertholf received orders to attend the Naval War College in Newport, Rhode Island, to audit the course convening there on 1 June. On the specified date, Bertholf reported to Capt. H. C. Taylor, USN, the commandant of Naval Station Newport and the president of the Naval War College. Bertholf was the first Revenue-Cutter Service officer to attend the college. He was joined there by twenty-five U.S. Navy officers, one officer of the Rhode Island Naval Militia, and one officer from the Danish navy.

The four and a half months Bertholf spent at the Naval War College proved to be among the most important of his early career. The people he met and the knowledge he gained of naval war tactics would be extremely valuable to him later in his career. Students of the college heard distinguished lecturers in the fields of naval strategy, naval history, and international relations. In addition to these lectures Bertholf also learned by participating in war games, tactical exercises, and steam-launch exercises. A good deal of his learning was at his own initiative.

The lecturers at the Naval War College included Alfred Thayer Mahan, who taught that sea power was often the decisive factor in a campaign or an entire war. The tall, balding, and ascetic-looking Mahan was not a typical naval officer. For one thing, he had been born at West Point to a faculty member at the Military Academy. Rather than follow the obvious course and join the army, Mahan obtained an appointment to the Naval Academy. Because he had previously attended Columbia College for two years, Mahan was allowed to enter the third-year class, the last man in the school's history to be permitted to skip plebe (fourth-class) year. He graduated second in the Naval Academy's class of 1859 and served on blockade duty and as an instructor at the academy during the Civil War. Mahan had joined the faculty of the Naval War College when it opened in 1885 and was its second president, succeeding Stephen Luce, from 1886 to 1889. Mahan's compilation of his lectures at the War College, published in 1890 as *The Influence of Sea Power upon History, 1660–1783*, brought international fame both to himself and to the Naval War College and rekindled American interest in sea power. The book quickly found favor in Britain as well, where Mahan received honorary degrees from Oxford and Cambridge. It was translated into Japanese and German. Indeed, Kaiser Wilhelm II, who read the work in 1894, had a translation placed in every German navy ship and in the libraries of all major civil institutions in Germany.

Bertholf also interacted with Philo N. McGiffen, a member of the Naval Academy's class of 1882 about whom he had heard a great deal during his year at Annapolis. McGiffen graduated a few months before

Bertholf arrived, but his pranks and disciplinary problems while he was a naval cadet were already legendary. Prevented from pursuing a career in the U.S. Navy by the commissioning restrictions enacted by the Personnel Act of 1882, McGiffen offered his services to the Imperial Chinese Navy and was appointed a professor of seamanship and gunnery at the Chinese Naval Academy at Tientsin (Tianjin). McGiffen was promoted to commander within a few years and served as adviser to the captain of the seven-thousand-ton battleship *Chen Yuen*, the sister ship of the *Ting Yuen*, the flagship of Admiral Ting. During the Battle of Yalu in September 1894, McGiffen assumed command of the battleship when the captain fled the bridge early in the battle. The *Chen Yuen* took more than 150 hits during the engagement and was on fire eight different times, but McGiffen's skillful maneuvering of the vessel protected the Chinese flagship and enabled the two Chinese battleships to withstand an attack by the main enemy squadron until the Japanese force steamed away. Badly wounded in the battle, McGiffen had to resign from the Chinese navy and return to New York City for treatment. An obviously talented officer, McGiffen was, ironically, the first American to command a modern armored battleship in action. He shared his firsthand insights on this first major sea fight of the battleship era with Bertholf and his classmates at Newport.

In addition to these lecturers already well known to Bertholf by reputation, he met two others he would deal with again later in his career. Lt. Albert Niblack lectured on signaling and its relationship to naval tactics. During World War I, Rear Admiral Niblack would command the American naval forces at Gibraltar, which would include several Coast Guard cutters. Mr. Charlemagne Tower lectured on "Earl Cornwallis and His Connection with the American War." Bertholf would next encounter Tower in 1901 in Saint Petersburg, where the historian was serving as the U.S. ambassador to Imperial Russia.

On 15 October 1895, trained in the principles of strategy and with a broadened knowledge of naval history and tactics, Bertholf became the first Revenue-Cutter Service officer to complete the course of the Naval War College. Among other things, the course had emphasized the necessity of constant training for officers in ship handling and squadron maneuvers, crucial knowledge for Revenue-Cutter Service officers during wartime, when they operated in U.S. Navy squadrons.

After completing the course at the Naval War College, Bertholf was assigned temporary duty as the executive officer of the USRC *Manhattan*.

The brief assignment offered a welcome opportunity to spend time with his newly widowed mother. Based in New York harbor, the *Manhattan,* a 102-foot harbor tug, operated on the Hudson River as well as in Long Island Sound.

In the latter part of November Bertholf traveled to the Brusstan Ship-building Company in Baltimore to report aboard the USRC *Chase* as the executive officer of both the ship and the School of Instruction. As the executive officer, Bertholf was second in command and the alter ego of the commanding officer/superintendent. He took precedence over all other officers on the *Chase* and was responsible for the organization, performance of duty, good order, and discipline of both the *Chase's* crew and the embarked cadets.

Major changes were under way both aboard the *Chase* and in the Revenue-Cutter Service as a whole when Bertholf reported aboard. In the 1880s, the U.S. Navy, struggling with the problem of a surplus of graduates from its academy, had suggested closing the Revenue-Cutter Service School of Instruction and using the Naval Academy as the source of Revenue-Cutter Service officers. In 1890 the navy finally succeeded in closing the School of Instruction and began placing Annapolis graduates (usually from the lower end of the class) in officers' billets in the Revenue-Cutter Service. For the next four years, the officer corps of the Revenue-Cutter Service was augmented by Annapolis graduates, who continued to wear U.S. Navy uniforms and knew little of customs matters or maritime law enforcement—and apparently cared less. Most considered the assignment demeaning.

Rescue for the service came in the person of Grover Cleveland. In 1893 Cleveland had returned to the White House for his second (but nonconsecutive) term. Although he was a strong champion of increased naval construction, Cleveland was not in favor of closing the Revenue-Cutter Service School of Instruction. In 1894 he restored the defunct school to life. A new class of cadets was assembled, the *Chase* was recommissioned, and a training cruise was conducted that summer.

An act of Congress passed in 1895 retired many inactive older Revenue-Cutter Service officers occupying senior billets in "awaiting orders" status. The retirement of these senior officers broke the promotion log-jam, and the service soon found itself without any third lieutenants. The need for additional junior officers suddenly became urgent. The *Chase* was too small to meet these demands for young officers, but the nation was in an economic depression and there was no money for a new school ship. The Revenue-Cutter Service adopted an ingenious solution. The *Chase* was temporarily decommissioned and sent to a Baltimore shipyard, where it was cut into two pieces and lengthened amidships by forty feet. This transformation was in full swing when Bertholf reported aboard. The enlargement increased the *Chase's* capacity in cadet steerage from thirteen to twenty-five without adversely affecting the ship's sailing characteristics.

This was not the only change aboard the *Chase* since Bertholf had graduated in 1887. The vessel now flew the national ensign in addition to the revenue cutter ensign. In the summer of 1895 Capt. Charles F. Shoemaker, chief of the Revenue Marine Division at the Treasury Department, directed all revenue cutters to display the national ensign at the main peak or flagstaff aft. The revenue ensign prescribed by law would henceforth be flown from the foretruck as a distinguishing flag.

The course of instruction had changed significantly since Bertholf's time as a cadet as well. Young men entering the school from civilian life now had to have a college education before they could be appointed as cadets, the idea being that their educational requirements would be practically completed prior to appointment, leaving the entire probationary term of two years aboard the *Chase* open for instruction in the technical aspects of the profession. As a result, the curriculum now included only professional and technical subjects directly related to the seagoing arts and revenue cutter work, all taught by the ship's officers. The new course of study was designed to be a far more advanced course than the one Bertholf had followed.

With all the shipyard work completed, the *Chase* was placed back in commission at noon on 8 February 1896 under the command of Capt. Oscar C. Hamlet. The enrollment of the School of Instruction had more than doubled in size. Among the entering class of cadets was Charles Satterlee, who would later be the commanding officer of the USCGC *Tampa* when it was lost with all hands in World War I.

The School of Instruction now entered what Coast Guard Academy histories often call "the gypsy years."[1] The *Chase* had no permanent homeport and returned to New Bedford only for occasional casual visits. The period of cadet instruction was spent almost entirely at sea. The *Chase* cruised for seven months in the spring and summer and spent the winter months in southern ports such as Wilmington, Charleston, Key

West, Tampa, Pensacola, and Mobile. During four of those months, instruction was devoted to work in port with occasional practice under way. The cadets were granted leave during the remaining month while the vessel underwent its annual overhauling, cleaning, and painting.

Fourteen members of the class of 1898 reported in January. These first cadets under the new system included three former naval cadets from Annapolis and one from West Point. On 12 March the *Chase* sailed for Bermuda, arriving on 25 March. While in Bermuda, Bertholf and the other *Chase* officers paid a visit to HMS *Rambler*. After a two-week visit the *Chase* sailed back to Baltimore, leaving Bermuda on 10 April and arriving home on 23 April. While outward bound to Bermuda the *Chase* had received orders to go on a practice cruise during July, August, September, and October 1896.

In June, nine new members of the class of 1898 arrived in Baltimore and reported aboard the *Chase,* which was then anchored off Canton Hollow. William J. Wheeler, one of the nine, remembered that as soon as they were settled in their staterooms, two to a room, the new cadets were called to the cabin for an interview with Captain Hamlet, the commanding officer. Captain Hamlet gave them a sensible talk in which he set the ground rules. The *Chase* lay at anchor in Canton Hollow for about a week while sails were being bent and other preparations were made for the practice cruise. Second Lieutenant Bertholf, the executive officer, oversaw daily boat drills. In addition to being on deck practically all day assisting in sending up and bending sails, the cadets also had four hours of deck watch each night.[2]

On 24 June the harbor cutter *W. H. Crawford* towed the school ship out of the harbor and the *Chase* set sail for Boston, arriving on the evening of 2 July. The vessel anchored to await daybreak, which came on with a strong headwind blowing. Without hesitation Captain Hamlet got the *Chase* under way and tacked up the channel through the Narrows to an anchorage off the New England docks in Boston. It had been many years since a square-rigger had stood up to the Boston wharves against a headwind, and the ship excited a great deal of favorable comment from the newspapers and the sailors of the area. The *Chase* remained in Boston for a few weeks, during which time drills and studies were carried out with diligence.

On 24 July the *Chase* received orders to sail to Gibraltar and Funchal, Madeira, returning in time to reach Tampa, Florida, by 30 November.

On 17 August the *Chase* sailed from Boston and the annual practice cruise began. When the ship arrived in Gibraltar on 12 September, the usual gun salute was fired and returned. On the fourteenth the U.S. Naval Academy's school ship *Saratoga* arrived. Bertholf assisted Captain Hamlet in welcoming the *Saratoga*'s commanding officer when he paid his official call. On the seventeenth Bertholf welcomed the governor of Gibraltar aboard the *Chase*.

After a week in Gibralter and a brief visit to Funchal the *Chase* sailed for Tampa Bay via Saint Thomas, Virgin Islands, where the school ship made a brief stay after arriving on 25 November. On leaving Saint Thomas the *Chase* was caught in the tail of a hurricane of moderate intensity. The *Chase* drove before the storm for several days, logging approximately eleven knots with the sail area reduced to a minimum, and arrived off Port Tampa on 14 December. After a few days at Port Tampa the *Chase* sailed across Tampa Bay to Saint Petersburg on 20 December, arriving that same day at what was then a village of three thousand. After three months of winter port study at the wharf at Saint Petersburg the *Chase* departed on 10 April 1897, arriving in Pensacola three days later. On 17 April the school ship sailed for Charleston, South Carolina, arriving at 9:30 P.M. on 29 April.

On 5 May the *Chase* sailed for Hampton Roads, Virginia, and then Baltimore, Maryland. At 1:40 A.M. the next day, about fifty miles east of the Charleston Bar, the *Chase* collided with the *Richard F. C. Hartley,* a large schooner out of Boston. When Bertholf scrambled on deck in the darkness, he discovered that the head booms, foretop mast, and main topgallant mast had been carried away. The *Chase* had the right-of-way under the Rules of the Road, and the schooner was clearly at fault. The *Chase* limped back into Charleston under its own sails on 8 May after declining numerous offers of tows. The USRC *Morrill* towed the *Chase* from Charleston as far as Southport. From there the *Chase* was towed the rest of the way to Baltimore by the USRC *Windom,* arriving at 1:00 P.M. on 29 May. The cadets were granted two months' leave while the *Chase* underwent repairs.

In August the newly repaired *Chase* was ordered on a practice cruise to New England. About a week before the *Chase* got under way on 28 August, however, Lieutenant Bertholf was detached for special duty with the Life-Saving Service. Another noteworthy event occurred at the end of that summer. In September, Wallace Bertholf, one of Ellsworth's younger brothers, entered the Naval Academy in Annapolis. Their mother would now have two sons serving in the naval services of the United States. Wallace stayed the course, graduated from the Naval Academy on 7 June 1901, and went on to a distinguished career in the navy. He was awarded the Navy Cross for distinguished service while commanding the USS *Harrisburg* in the hazardous duty of transporting troops and supplies to European ports during World War I.

In November Bertholf received orders that would have far-reaching consequences for his career. He was ordered to report for duty on the USRC *Bear,* which served on the Bering Sea Patrol. The cutter had already become a legend for delivering Siberian reindeer to the native Alaskans, protecting seal rookeries, and serving as an ad hoc Alaskan territorial courtroom. Although he did not know it at the time, his new assignment would provide Ellsworth Bertholf with the opportunity of a lifetime—the opportunity to become a national hero.

❧ 4 ❧

THE OVERLAND
RELIEF EXPEDITION

I n the spring of 1897 Seattle was the booming collection and jump-
ing-off point for the Klondike gold rush in Canada. When the
USRC *Bear* returned from the Bering Sea and arrived at its homeport in Seattle on 6 November 1897, 2d Lieutenant Bertholf was waiting.
He boarded the ship and reported to Capt. Francis Tuttle, who in the
spring of 1896 had replaced the legendary Capt. "Hell Roaring" Michael
A. Healy as the commanding officer. Bertholf was proud that he had
been assigned to a ship that had already played such an important role
in shaping the history of Alaska.

Bertholf's new vessel was a steam barkentine built in Scotland in 1874
and designed for working in heavy ice. As he inspected his new ship
belowdecks, he would have noticed the *Bear*'s special construction. Its
keel, ribs, and hull planking were oak. The ribs were exceptionally heavy
for a ship of only 190 feet, and were closer together than they would have
been on a vessel designed for service in ice-free waters. The *Bear*'s oak
planking was six inches thick, steamed and bent to fit the ribs, and fas-
tened tightly with the best Swedish iron. Bulkheads, beams, and braces
crisscrossed the interior of the hull to strengthen the ship—to make it,
in fact, a sailing battering ram. Bertholf would also have inspected the
enlisted men's cramped quarters in the forward part of the ship, deroga-
torily referred to as the "glory hole."[1]

37

Aft of the crew's quarters were the rooms where the engine and boiler were bolted to steel bedplates that were firmly attached to the ship's frame. The engine was connected to a two-bladed propeller at the end of a movable shaft. The shaft was rigged so that the propeller could be raised under the stern and repaired while at sea. The propeller and rudder are a ship's most vulnerable parts in ice-strewn water, and the ability to raise them out of the water also helped to prevent damage to the screw from pack ice.

Walking about topside on his new vessel, Bertholf might have noticed that the fore and mizzen masts were of Norway pine, while the mainmast was a 127-foot tube of iron. The decks were teak. Ironwood from Australia sheathed the oak-planked hull to protect it from jagged ice floes. The *Bear's* bow, enfolded in steel plates, was designed to withstand the impact when it rammed thick ice. As a trained mariner Bertholf would doubtless have understood that the *Bear* was in no sense an icebreaker, but it was able to withstand the crushing and battering that went along with following leads in ice fields because of its unusually heavy oak framing and planking and its ironwood sheathing.

He also probably soon discovered that in addition to its sturdy construction the ship was remarkably self-sustaining for its size, with ample capacity for coal, water, and supplies for lengthy cruises. This fact, together with a simple and reliable propelling plant and an adequate sail area, enabled the *Bear* to remain for long periods away from supply and repair bases.

Also waiting for the *Bear* that day were waterfront officials with news of Arctic whalers trapped in the ice at Point Barrow. The fall of 1897 had come exceptionally early and had caught eight whaling vessels unprepared in far northern waters. The whalers had expected to reach San Francisco early in the winter, and none carried enough supplies to see them through the winter. The nearly three hundred officers and crewmen of the eight vessels in the whaling fleet would probably perish from hunger unless relief could reach them.

The Chamber of Commerce and people of San Francisco appealed to President McKinley for assistance. Sending a ship into the Arctic at that time of year was unheard of, but the number of lives in peril necessitated the attempt. After thoroughly discussing the subject with his advisers at a cabinet meeting, the president decided to assign the task of getting help to the trapped men to the Revenue-Cutter Service, whose officers were experienced in Arctic duty. Advised that no other suitable government vessel could be made available for the rescue, President McKinley and Secretary of the Treasury Lyman J. Gage directed the *Bear* to prepare to go to Point Barrow to rescue the stranded whalers.

Bertholf's first few days aboard the *Bear* were busy ones. While he was familiarizing himself with his new ship he also had to carry out his responsibilities as one of the ship's officers helping to oversee the crew as it prepared the *Bear* for the expedition. Preparations began on 11 November. The ship's holds and decks were quickly loaded with provisions for the stranded whalers and with dogs and sleds for overland travel. William Schultz, a crewman on the *Bear* who reported aboard about the same time as Bertholf, noted that "the people of San Francisco had donated canned foods, sheepskin clothing and cases and cases of eggs. There was no refrigeration on the *Bear,* of course, and we later had to dump the eggs overboard."[2] The *Bear* was soon fully provisioned with one year's rations for the crew plus an additional twelve thousand rations as relief stores for the imperiled whalers. Bertholf was amazed that an expedition could be fitted out for a year's absence in the Arctic in such an incredibly short time.[3]

On 29 November, three weeks after arriving back in Seattle, the *Bear,* carrying an all-volunteer crew, steamed at full speed through the forest-lined Strait of Juan de Fuca and headed north. As Bertholf soon discovered, however, speed was not one of the *Bear*'s virtues. Under favorable conditions the ship's compound engine might drive it along at eight knots per hour, but with a strong headwind, two or three knots was the maximum speed attainable. Under sail alone the ship often made seven knots, and under sail and steam in favorable conditions, nine knots. The *Bear* also rolled so badly that those accustomed to larger vessels were invariably seasick during their first storm aboard. The rolling likely presented no problem to Lieutenant Bertholf, who was accustomed to sailing on small revenue cutters.

In these days before gold was discovered in Alaska, no vessel of the *Bear*'s size had ever been in the waters it now entered, and no ship of any size had been there at this time of the year. Only smaller whaling ships came here, and then only in the summer months. It was fully understood that the *Bear* could not, even under the most favorable conditions of ice navigation in that region, reach Point Barrow before July or August. The only way to bring food to the stranded whalers was to drive reindeer herds overland to them. The reindeer would supply enough food to keep the men alive until the *Bear* arrived with the rest of the supplies the following summer. Bertholf was among the officers aboard the *Bear* who volunteered for the overland relief expedition.

By 10 December, when the *Bear* reached Unalaska, Captain Tuttle had decided to send his executive officer, 1st Lt. David H. Jarvis; 2d Lieutenant Bertholf; and the *Bear*'s surgeon, Dr. Samuel J. Call, overland to rescue the whalers. All three of the men had volunteered. Jarvis, who was to command the expedition, had served eight seasons in the Arctic Ocean on the *Bear,* was familiar with the coast, and knew the natives well. Bertholf considered it his good fortune to be among those selected for the expedition. Here was a chance for adventure and heroics, a chance to prove his courage and endurance.

On 14 December 1897 the *Bear* reached 63 degrees, 13 minutes, north latitude, 167 degrees, 28 minutes, west longitude, about twenty-five miles northeast of Saint Lawrence Island and about eighty-five miles from Cape Nome. At that point the ice became so thick that the *Bear* could proceed no further. Unfortunately, drift ice prevented the *Bear* from landing the rescue party at that location, which would have saved them about seven hundred miles of travel on land. Captain Tuttle had no choice but to head back south to Cape Vancouver to land the overland expedition.

On 16 December 1897 Bertholf and the two other members of the expedition were hastily landed with their supplies near the village of Tununak on Nelson Island, near Cape Vancouver. After the party's provisions, clothing, and camping gear were safely on the beach, Bertholf watched the ship's boat return to the *Bear,* wondering whether he would ever see his shipmates again. The *Bear* turned toward Dutch Harbor, Unalaska, its home base for the winter of 1897–98, leaving Bertholf and the other members of the rescue party on their own. The plan was to proceed overland as far as Cape Prince of Wales, where several herds of domestic reindeer might be found. After that, the party would battle the Arctic winter as they attempted to reach the icebound whalers fifteen hundred miles away.

The only mode of transportation in Alaska during the winter was by dogsled. With that in mind, the party proceeded to Tununak to pack their sleds and harness the dogs. Natives from the nearby village came to meet them in kayaks and transported the supplies and equipment to the village. Bertholf and the others walked the four miles and arrived

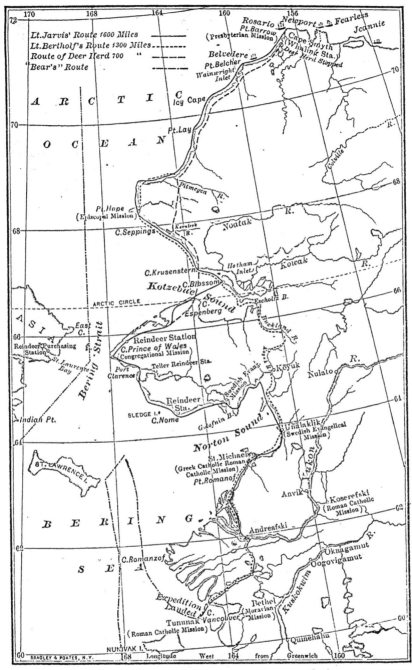

Route of the overland relief expedition to Point Barrow, Alaska
From Harper's New Monthly Magazine 99 (June 1899)

shortly after their supplies. Bertholf discovered that a Russian trader who lived in the village owned not only the dogs but also everything else there. Arrangements were made for the trader to take the rescue party as far as Saint Michaels, where they counted on obtaining fresh dogs to continue the journey.

After spending a day completing the arrangements and packing the sleds, Bertholf and the others departed early on the morning of 18 December. Each member of the party had a sled pulled by a team of seven dogs harnessed in pairs with the leader in front. Each of them also had an Inuit helper. Bertholf was quickly initiated into the mysteries of sled travel. He discovered that rather than sitting in the sled and being pulled by the dogs, sled travel consisted mostly of pushing the sled from behind, especially when going uphill.

Instead of traveling along the coast from Tununak to Saint Michaels, where the Russian trader told them the road was apt to be very rough, they headed out across the countryside toward the Yukon River at Andreafski. Native villages were scattered along the route, and the rescue party hoped to reach one every night. Camping would be easier near a village, and they might be able to get fresh dogs if any of theirs gave out.

On the very first day, the party had to cross a range of mountains more than fifteen hundred feet in height. In some places the rise was so steep that it required three or four members of the party to help the dogs pull each sled. When Bertholf reached the summit, he was discouraged to see another mountain before him, higher and steeper than the one he had just ascended, with a deep valley in between. He soon forgot to worry about the next climb in the excitement of the descent into the valley. The dogs were unharnessed while he and the others prepared to coast down on the sleds. Bertholf was familiar with tobogganing, but that was tame sport indeed compared with this. As it picked up momentum, the heavy sled seemed to fly. The exhilarating descent put Bertholf and the others in good spirits again, and they started for the second mountain with a more positive attitude, knowing they had a coasting to look forward to after the ascent.

After that first day they were not troubled by any more mountains. Their route now led across the Yukon River delta, which consisted mainly of frozen swamps and small streams. Bertholf was amazed that the Inuit guides knew which way to go. There was no trail visible to him, and the guides never seemed to consult the party's small pocket compasses.

On the third day they reached the village of Ki-yi-lieug-a-mute, where the Russian trader informed the rescue party that some of the dogs were too young to stand further travel. He had hoped to replace his dogs with dogs from the village, but those dogs were away and were not expected to return for two days. Lieutenant Jarvis decided to take two of the good teams and go on ahead with Dr. Call and two of the native guides. Bertholf was instructed to follow as soon as possible.

Early the next morning the provisions and outfits were divided, and Bertholf bid Jarvis and Call farewell. Because the advance party had taken the only tent, Bertholf had to sleep in one of the native huts. The body heat from the dozen or so inmates of each hut would be sufficient to make the temperature inside quite comfortable. The odor produced by decaying fish, ancient seal blubber and oil, and the natives themselves, who, understandably, were not regular bathers, was another matter. Bertholf selected a hut at random and began accustoming himself to the smell by going inside for a few minutes at a time throughout the day, each time remaining a little longer. He thus was able to imagine that he was comfortable when he crawled into his sleeping bag that night.

Two days later the village's dogs returned as expected, and on 27 December Bertholf left Ki-yi-lieug-a-mute and headed for Andreafski, one of the trading stations of the Alaska Commercial Company. When he reached Saint Michaels at about noon on 1 January, Bertholf found that Jarvis had departed only a few hours before his arrival, leaving Bertholf a letter of instructions. The letter informed Bertholf that Jarvis was on his way to Cape Prince of Wales, where he would start herds of reindeer in that vicinity on their way up the coast. Since there was no chance to get provisions between Cape Prince of Wales and Point Hope, Bertholf was to go to Unalakleet and transport one thousand pounds of supplies that had been purchased there to Kotzebue Sound. From there he was instructed to proceed to Cape Blossom, where he would meet Jarvis and the deer herd.

Bertholf headed for Unalakleet on 6 January. Although the town was only sixty miles from Saint Michaels, the trip took Bertholf and his party three days. Their progress was slowed by an exceedingly rough trail strewn with rocks and boulders of all sizes. On the evening of the eighth they pulled into Unalakleet, a village with a native population of about two hundred, a Swedish mission school, and an Alaska Commercial Company trading station. By this time of the winter, the thermometer reached only 35–40 degrees below zero during the day.

Bertholf had hoped to obtain new dogs at Unalakleet, but there were none to be had. When the dogs had not arrived by the fifteenth, he decided to go on to Koyuk at the head of Norton Sound, taking the provisions he could manage with his one team. Bertholf arrived at Koyuk on 19 January, having picked up no dogs along the way. While they were at Koyuk, Bertholf's interpreter informed him that the Inuits in the party were demanding an increase in their pay. With no other means of transportation available, Bertholf had to agree.

From Koyuk, Bertholf's party headed on toward Cape Blossom. For the most part they passed through gently rolling country devoid of trees or shrubbery except along the rivers, where they found brush in abundance and some scrubby pine trees. Because the snow was very deep and soft, the party members had to wear snowshoes nearly all the time, and often had to tramp back and forth ahead of the dog teams to pack the snow down for them. They did not reach Cape Blossom until the evening of 11 February.

Meanwhile, Jarvis and Call, traveling light, had pushed on from Unalakleet and proceeded along the coast to Cape Prince of Wales, assembling a large herd of reindeer from various stations along the way. Bertholf welcomed Jarvis and Call when they arrived at Cape Blossom on the twelfth. He had not seen them since 20 December, and they sat up far into the night exchanging stories about their experiences.

On 15 February Jarvis left for Point Hope, leaving Bertholf behind with provisions for the reindeer herders and instructions to follow with the herd as soon as it arrived. With nothing but empty expanses of snow and ice to look at, Bertholf anticipated a very tiresome wait. He was very glad when W. T. Lopp of the American Missionary Society arrived on the eighteenth. Lopp explained that he had crossed the ice with the reindeer herd from Cape Espenberg to Cape Krusenstern, where he found a letter from Jarvis telling him to find Bertholf at Cape Blossom and bring him to Cape Krusenstern. He left the reindeer behind to rest and came to Cape Blossom with dog teams. Since Bertholf had returned all his dog teams to their owners, they loaded their provisions on Bertholf's reindeer sleds and Lopp's dogsleds. Bertholf and Lopp reached Krusenstern on the nineteenth and remained until the twenty-first to allow the reindeer much-needed rest, and then started along the coast toward Point Good Hope.

When they reached the mouth of the Kivalena River, Lopp and Bertholf parted ways. Lopp was to take the deer herd inland, avoiding the long journey around Point Hope. Bertholf was to procure more dogsleds and proceed to Point Hope, where, according to his instructions, he was to meet Jarvis again. When Bertholf reached Cape Seppings, he learned that Jarvis had gone back to the Kivalena to meet Lopp. Bertholf decided to wait where he was until Jarvis returned, then the two men proceeded to Point Hope, arriving on 2 March.

Since there was a large store of flour and other provisions at Liebes's whaling station there, Jarvis decided that Bertholf should remain at Point Hope to oversee all matters relating to the relief expedition and to provide assistance to any of the shipwrecked men Jarvis might send back from Point Barrow. Bertholf was thankful when Mr. Nelson, the manager of the whaling station, offered accommodations in his own cabin. He had had enough of the overpowering odors of whale blubber and dead seal.

Having replenished their supplies, Jarvis and Call set out again on 4 March. They reached Point Barrow on the twenty-ninth, and the government herd of four hundred reindeer arrived a few days later, bringing the stranded whalers the first square meal they had seen for several months. In the meantime, Bertholf made a side trip up the coast from Point Hope as far as the Pitmega River, where he cached provisions and dog food for the use of anyone who might be coming down the coast. Lopp, anxious to get back to his family, returned to his home at Cape Prince of Wales.

During its early decades as an American possession, Alaska was a special charge of the Revenue-Cutter Service, which acted as a kind of liaison between the parent government at Washington and its territorial offspring. While some have called the Revenue-Cutter Service officers who served in Alaska the "American Mounties," others have seen them as being "more like the historically famous itinerant justices of Angevin England—extended arms of the state, reaching out to preserve peace and administer justice in those far-away regions where the authority of the government had not yet penetrated."[4] It was thus not unusual that Jarvis, once the relief operation had been successfully concluded, directed Bertholf to destroy the illicit stills in the area and to investigate two recent murders, collecting evidence and taking such action as he deemed necessary for apprehending the murderers.

Revenue-Cutter Service officers were not rigid teetotalers inspired by Carrie Nation and sworn to battle "demon rum." Alcohol was particularly deadly in Alaska. The Inuit people faced a continuous struggle for existence, and the hunter who pursued the joys of the bottle and neglected to prepare for the winter would soon be dead, along with his wife and children. Bertholf visited the villages in the area and searched all the houses for stills. After he warned the villagers about the bad effects of whiskey, many led him to stills buried in the snow. Bertholf found and destroyed twenty stills during his time at Point Hope. He believed, however, that many others remained undiscovered, and that even if they were all destroyed, the natives could easily make more. Bertholf concluded that the illicit distilling would stop only if outside traders were prevented from supplying molasses and sugar to the natives or if these items were diluted with something that would inhibit fermentation.

Since the *Bear* and its officers symbolized U.S. government authority in Alaska, Bertholf had also been directed to investigate two murders. The first incident he looked into had occurred in August 1897 when a young Inuit man belonging to the Cape Prince of Wales village shot and killed a white prospector by the name of Frank Boyd while the latter was on his way up the Noatuk River on a prospecting trip. Bertholf was convinced that the murder had been committed to avenge the death of the young man's father, who had been killed some years before by white men onboard a trading vessel during a fight between the vessel's crew and the natives of Cape Prince of Wales. In his report on the murder, Bertholf was careful to defend the Inuit people. "I do not intend to convey by the above the idea that the Eskimo is murderous by nature," he wrote. "Far from that being the case, he is, as a race, unusually gentle, kind, and good natured; but even among the best tempered of people quarrels will sometimes occur and then if a killing takes place the feud which ensues may cause the death of others in the course of several years."[5]

The other murder Bertholf investigated had taken place the previous May near Cape Thompson. An Inuit man had shot and killed his former wife because she refused to return to live with him and his new wife. Bertholf expected to arrest the accused murderer and take him aboard the *Bear* for transportation to stand trial, but he discovered that the accused had died from an illness a little more than a month after committing the murder.

When Bertholf returned to Point Hope in March, the landscape was one vast expanse of snow in all directions. It remained that way until the summer, when the sun finally rose above the horizon and stayed there, and the snow rapidly disappeared. By the latter part of July there was not a sign of snow anywhere except on the tops of the highest mountains. Bertholf was amazed at how quickly the flowers began to bloom. It was difficult for him to believe then that he was 125 miles north of the Arctic Circle.

Finally able to leave its winter port in Unalaska, the *Bear* reached Point Hope on 15 July. Bertholf was glad to see the ship and his shipmates again after a separation of more than six months. He came aboard and gave Captain Tuttle all the news he had about the expedition. The news Captain Tuttle offered in exchange, however, was far more interesting. Bertholf was astonished to learn that the United States was at war with Spain and that Commodore Dewey had won a glorious victory at Manila.

The *Bear*, with Bertholf onboard, left Point Hope on the sixteenth and worked its way through the drift ice as far as Point Lay, where it anchored in response to signals from the shore. Soon afterward a canoe came alongside, and Captain Sherman of the *Orca* and some members of the other wrecked vessels came onboard. They had come down the coast to bring a letter from Jarvis to Captain Tuttle telling him the situation at Point Barrow. Heavy ice prevented the *Bear* from steaming any farther north. On the twenty-fifth the ice opened up a little and the *Bear* was able to get as far as Wainwright Inlet. On 28 July the *Bear* made fast to ground-ice at Cape Smyth, opposite the whaling station where most of the whalers stranded at Point Barrow had taken refuge.

With the *Bear*'s arrival, the whalers' eleven-month ordeal came to an end. The overland relief party had distributed 12,481 pounds of reindeer meat, which surely helped them to survive. When Jarvis and later Dr. Call came out on the ice, Bertholf gave both men a hearty welcome. In the excitement of the war news, however, everyone soon forgot the shipwrecked whalers and the long, hard winter now past. The only events worth discussing were the war and the Battle of Manila.

By the following day most of the shipwrecked whalers had come aboard the *Bear*, anxious to leave their winter home for good. But a westerly wind jammed pack ice against the vessel, preventing it from leaving. On 3 August the wind shifted to the southwest, pushing the pack ice against the ship with so much pressure that the port side of the *Bear* was pushed inward a few inches. For a few minutes, everyone onboard feared the worst, but fortunately the pressure eased before any real damage was done. The danger was not over, however, for with the wind blowing onshore, it was sure to happen again, and the next time the *Bear* might not be so lucky. Hasty preparations were made to abandon ship should it become necessary. For the next few days Bertholf went to sleep expecting to be called at any time, and every morning gave a sigh of relief to find the good old ship still safe.

On 15 August the wind shifted to the east and began moving the pack ice offshore. About noon on the next day the *Bear,* after sixteen days as a prisoner of the ice, forced its way through the remaining pack ice. Bertholf joined the crew in a rousing cheer when they found themselves in open water again. The *Bear* steamed southward carrying ninety-three officers and men of the wrecked whaling vessels. At Point Hope they picked up nine more destitute seamen and turned for home.

The *Bear* steamed into Seattle at 11:00 A.M. on 13 September 1898 after an absence of nine and a half months and received an international ovation for its rescue of the whalers. The overland relief expedition was hailed as—and still is considered—one of the greatest Arctic rescues of all time. The *Bear* became the first ship in history to sail into the Arctic in winter. Bertholf attributed the fact that no lives were lost in the rescue party to their caution and good judgment rather than to mere good luck.

Bertholf had faced and overcome perhaps the greatest challenge of his life. He had endured three and a half months of Arctic travel in the midst of winter. Exhaustion, darkness, and gale-force winds had been routine. Many times he had crawled into his sleeping bag hungry because the weather or lack of fuel rendered cooking impossible. Running, walking, and pushing behind a sled through deep snow and over rough and difficult trails of broken ice for more than thirteen hundred miles was indescribably fatiguing. The thermometer had registered as much as 50 degrees below zero during his travels. But Bertholf had met the challenges and emerged victorious.

On the voyage home from the Arctic, Bertholf and his fellow officers and crew members had excitedly discussed the part they and the *Bear* might play in the war. They were greatly disappointed when they learned that the United States and Spain had agreed to a peace settlement while their ship was still fast in the ice off Point Barrow. The men could only listen enviously to accounts of the victory of Dewey's command at Manila Bay, where the cutter *McCulloch* had acted as the dispatch boat; of the gallant activities of the cutter *Manning* along the coasts of Cuba; and the of defeat of Cevera by the White Squadron off Santiago, with Commodore Schley, a former commander of the *Bear,* playing a leading role. Bertholf more than likely swelled with pride for the Revenue-Cutter Service when he learned that the cutter *Hudson,* disdaining the point-blank fire of three Spanish gunboats and several shore batteries, had entered Cardenas harbor and towed the disabled and badly battered destroyer *Winslow* to sea and safety.

Bertholf also learned that the president had made all revenue cutters in the North Pacific a part of the U.S. Navy. This should have meant that he and his shipmates on the *Bear* were Spanish-American War veterans. Unfortunately, the executive order signed by President McKinley listed all the cutters in those waters by name except the *Bear.*

But Bertholf and his shipmates received their fair share of glory. Captain Tuttle, in his report to the secretary of the treasury on the cruise and expedition, recommended "that the heroic services of First Lieutenant D. H. Jarvis, Second Lieutenant E. P. Bertholf and Surgeon S. J. Call should meet with such recognition as the Department sees fit to bestow." So impressed was President McKinley with the rescue that crew members on the *Bear* were offered early discharges from the Revenue-Cutter Service as a reward.

Bertholf must have felt both pride and an enormous sense of accomplishment when he read President William McKinley's message to the Senate and House of Representatives of 17 January 1899:

> The hardships and perils encountered by the members of the overland expedition in their great journey through an almost uninhabited region, a barren waste of ice and snow, facing death itself every day for nearly four months, over a route never before traveled by white men, with no refuge but at the end of the journey, carrying relief and cheer to 275 distressed citizens of our country, all make another glorious page in the history of American seamen. They reflect by their heroic and gallant struggles the highest credit upon themselves and the Government which they faithfully served. I commend this heroic crew to the grateful consideration of Congress and the American people.
>
> The year just closed has been fruitful of noble achievements in the field of war; and while I have commended to your consideration the names of heroes who have shed luster upon the American name in valorous contests and battle by land and sea, it is no less my pleasure to invite your attention to a victory of peace the results of which cannot well be magnified, and the dauntless courage of the men engaged stamps them as true heroes, whose services cannot pass unrecognized.[6]

President McKinley went on to recommend that Congress vote a message of thanks to Capt. Francis Tuttle and the officers and men of the *Bear* "for their able and gallant services." Of even more significance for Lieutenant Bertholf, the commander in chief also recommended that "gold medals of honor of appropriate design, to be approved by the Secretary of the Treasury, be awarded to Lieutenants Jarvis and Bertholf and Dr. Call, commemorative of their heroic struggles in aid of suffering fellow-men." Responding to the president's recommendation, on 28 June 1902 Congress passed H.R. 11019, "An act directing the Sec'y of the Treasury to bestow medals upon First Lieut. David H. Jarvis, Second Lieut. Ellsworth P. Bertholf, and Samuel Call, Surgeon, all of the Revenue-Cutter Service."

To further ensure that his heroism would not be forgotten, Bertholf wrote an article for the June 1899 issue of *Harper's New Monthly Magazine* that included a map and numerous photographs in addition to a detailed description of the overland relief expedition. Besides bringing Bertholf lifelong fame, the overland relief expedition was one of the formative experiences of his life. For much of the expedition Bertholf had been separated from Lieutenant Jarvis, the expedition's leader, and forced to assume a great deal of responsibility. He had to make decisions about logistics, law enforcement, navigation, transportation, and many other issues by himself, and often in a harsh and hostile environment. He had to exercise initiative and judgment on a regular basis in very demanding situations. His role in the relief expedition gave him confidence in himself and in his abilities as a leader. Perhaps he may even have realized that if he could handle the challenges of the overland relief expedition, he could handle the challenges of just about any mission or any position. Events indicate that Bertholf never again doubted his ability to undertake greater responsibilities or face what might appear to be insurmountable challenges. Whenever a demanding task or position was available, Bertholf volunteered.

Bertholf as a naval cadet, U.S. Naval Academy, 1883
Courtesy of Bertholf family

New Quarters, U.S. Naval Academy, with the Tripoli Monument in the right foreground
Courtesy of Special Collections and Archives Division, Nimitz Library, U.S. Naval Academy

Bertholf as a cadet at the U.S. Revenue-Cutter Service School of Instruction, 1886
Courtesy of Bertholf family

USRC *Salmon P. Chase*
Courtesy of U.S. Coast Guard Archives

USRC *Levi Woodbury*
Courtesy of U.S. Naval Historical Center

USRC *Bear* arriving at Valdez, Alaska, 1908
Courtesy of U.S. Coast Guard Archives

Obverse of congressional gold medal of honor presented to Ellsworth
Bertholf
Courtesy of U.S. Coast Guard Archives

Reverse of congressional gold medal of honor presented to Ellsworth
Bertholf
Courtesy of U.S. Coast Guard Archives

Bertholf wearing his *shuba* in Saint Petersburg, Russia, 1901
Courtesy of Bertholf family

Captain Bertholf, USRCS, 1910
Courtesy of Bertholf family

USRC *Wissahickon*
Courtesy of U.S. Coast Guard Archives

USRC Seminole
Courtesy of U.S. Coast Guard Archives

❧ 5 ❧

GOLD, REINDEER, AND
BITTER COLD

Early in 1899, news spread that gold had been found on Anvil Creek near Cape Nome in Alaska. Gold had been discovered along the Klondike River in the Yukon Territory of Canada three years earlier, but the disorder that ensued there was a mere shadow of the chaos that characterized the Alaskan gold rush. The Royal Canadian Mounted Police maintained law and order throughout the Klondike gold rush, but there was no U.S. government authority present in Nome to bring order to the confusion. Gold, food, and a place to stay took precedence over everything else in this instant town. Disputes over claims abounded and were often settled at gunpoint. Even the first judge in the area ended up in jail. The army detachment in Saint Michael helped to keep things under control in its area, but the primary responsibility for policing the region fell to the Revenue-Cutter Service, which continued to be the primary U.S. government presence in Alaska.

Bertholf left the *Bear* in January 1899, shortly after it arrived in Seattle from the overland relief expedition, for a brief assignment in Washington, D.C., to write his account of the expedition. When that was completed, Bertholf was assigned to the USRC *Thetis*, which was then undergoing repairs at the Mare Island Naval Shipyard in San Francisco Bay. By coincidence, the *Bear* was also undergoing repairs at Mare Island that winter before sailing back to Seattle. Shortly after the *Bear* left the navy yard Bertholf received orders reassigning him to his old ship, but he had to travel all the way to Seattle to board it.

When the *Bear* arrived in Seattle on 11 May, Lieutenant Bertholf was waiting to reboard, this time as the executive officer. Capt. Francis Tuttle, the commanding officer of the *Bear* during the overland relief expedition, had become ill and Capt. David Jarvis had been assigned as the temporary commanding officer.

Before the *Bear* could go to Nome and try to establish order among the prospectors, there was one regular task to complete. The Revenue-Cutter Service had been importing Siberian reindeer into Alaska for the use of the Inuits, and another shipment was required. The *Bear* sailed from Port Townsend on 27 May and arrived at Dutch Harbor, Alaska, on 7 June. After coaling, the *Bear* sailed on to Petropavlovsk, Siberia, arriving on the seventeenth. The manager of the Russian Sealskin Company was contacted regarding the possibility of purchasing reindeer in that region. The *Bear's* officers had hoped to obtain as many reindeer there as the *Bear* could carry, but an epidemic had decimated the local herds and it was impossible to obtain any at all. The *Bear* headed north to Karaga Harbor on 23 June, arriving on the night of the twenty-sixth. There the ship's officers managed to contact the owners of a large herd, and on 6 and 7 July, 112 reindeer were purchased and taken onboard. The following day was spent gathering 285 bags of moss to feed the reindeer during the voyage to Alaska. The reindeer were off-loaded at Port Clarence on 14 July. Thirty had died during the voyage, many as a result of the rough voyage from Siberia.[1]

When the *Bear* finally reached Nome, or Anvil City, as it was still called then, the city was a seething, filthy, lawless mess. A large proportion of its population of twenty thousand people were living in crude shacks, tents, overturned boats, or any other shelter they could find. The population had an enormous turnover rate. Many of the gold seekers—cold, hungry, and with no place to stay—became discouraged and left the area, only to be replaced by newcomers still hopeful of finding riches in the gold fields.

When reports reached Nome of the suffering in the area north of the city, the *Bear* went there to investigate. At Kotzebue Sound, Lieutenant Bertholf and Surgeon Hawley were sent to examine the camp at Hotham Inlet, about twelve miles from the anchorage. They returned to the ship on the morning of 23 July with thirty-two sick people, then went back to Hotham Inlet and brought back all of those in a destitute condition—now a total of eighty-three persons. All would be transported back to Seattle.

The *Bear* checked in at Nome on the way to Seattle, and the officers and crew were amazed at what they found. What had been a wild city on their first visit was now complete bedlam. In less than two months the population had increased in size by a factor of ten. The *Bear* left for Seattle on 4 November, the last ship to leave Nome before it became ice-bound for the winter. The decks were crammed with luckless miners from Kotzebue Sound desperate to get back to the United States. In fact, they were among the lucky ones. Although their visions of instant riches had long since vanished, three thousand prospectors ignored the approach of winter and feverishly panned gravel as the *Bear* headed south. Many surely came to wish that they had been among those taken to Seattle on the *Bear*.

The eighty-three extra passengers stretched the ship's stores to the limit, yet at Saint Michael the *Bear* was forced to take more passengers onboard: several prisoners, a lunatic, a number of invalids, and two women wanted for smuggling. By the time they reached Seattle, the passengers and crew were reduced to eating dehydrated vegetables and dried fruit.

After landing the destitute passengers at Seattle, the *Bear* received from the USRC *McCulloch* three modern 6-pound Hotchkiss rifles to replace its outdated armament. After that, it was time for the ship to seek its winter quarters. En route to San Francisco, a keg was thrown over the side so that the *Bear*'s gun crews could have some much-needed target practice.

Lieutenant Bertholf helped guide the *Bear* through the Golden Gate on 11 November 1899. After off-loading all the assorted passengers and celebrating the turn of the century in San Francisco, the *Bear* departed on 7 January for San Diego, its new winter port, arriving on the tenth. There the crew labored under the tropical sun, stripping the ship of its masts and yards, knocking rust and scale from iron and steel with chipping hammers, and peeling away weather-beaten paint with scrapers. The *Bear* was virtually dismantled and dried out, and then reassembled, recoated, and rerigged. During the overhaul Bertholf traveled back to Washington, D.C., where he took and passed the examination for promotion to first lieutenant, with the promotion taking effect in June.

On 10 March the *Bear,* with Captain Tuttle once more in command, headed back to San Francisco, arriving four days later. After taking on and training some new crew members, the *Bear* sailed for the Bering Sea once again, departing on 25 April and arriving in Sitka on 14 May. Bertholf was no doubt impressed with this major city, which at that time was the capital of the U.S. Alaska Territory. Known as the "Paris of the Pacific" during its Russian days, the former political and commercial heart of Russian America featured the Russian bishop's house and Saint Michael's Russian Orthodox Cathedral.

As in the previous fall, the *Bear* rescued stranded gold seekers at Kotzebue Sound, this time taking them to Nome and Saint Michael rather than Seattle. The *Bear* arrived at Dutch Harbor on 23 May and commenced the summer's Bering Sea Patrol, arriving off Nome in early June.

The *Bear* had been at anchor off Nome for twenty-four hours when a severe gale began to blow. The storm drove the whaler *Alaska* onto the rocks, where it began to break up under the pounding waves. The whaler's crew refused to man the boats, preferring a delayed death to what they considered the suicide of trying to take a small boat through the surf to shore. It seemed certain that they would be lost when the ship broke up. The *Bear,* with both anchors down, chains paid out to their bitter ends, and humming under the strain, was itself in danger of being pushed onshore.

Captain Tuttle called for a volunteer boat crew to go to the rescue of the whalers. When all but one man stepped forward, Tuttle selected Bertholf to command the *Bear*'s whaleboat, which was launched into the angry sea. Bertholf got the boat clear of the *Bear* and went alongside the *Alaska.* Waves were cascading over the whaler, and Bertholf realized at once that the *Alaska* would not hold together long enough to make the several trips necessary to rescue the men in the *Bear*'s small boat. Bertholf and several members of his boat crew scrambled onboard the *Alaska.* Clinging to the rigging to keep from being washed overboard, they forced the whaler's crew into their own boats and launched them. Once set adrift, the whaler's crew rowed frantically toward the shore. Fortunately, the tug *Islam* was standing by at the edge of the surf to rescue the boats from peril and tow them out to the *Bear.* Bertholf and his men got back into their own boat and got away from the *Alaska* just before it started to break up. All hands had reached the *Bear*'s deck safely when the captain ordered the anchors raised and moved the ship from the exposed location into the lee of Sledge Island to wait out the storm. Bertholf had again proved his ability to make the right decisions and command men in potentially deadly situations.

Two days later the *Bear* returned to find the tent city at Nome half blown apart and the beaches swept clean in places. An army detachment finally arrived from Saint Michael to control the situation, allowing the *Bear* to leave for its Arctic patrol. Before leaving, however, Bertholf would distinguish himself in yet another heroic rescue. On the morning of 7 June, 2d Lieutenant Gamble and an ordinary seaman had been sent to the wreck of the *Alaska* to guard it until the whaler's master and crew could recover the cargo. Gamble had orders to remain onboard until relieved and was told that should the wind shift, the sea rise, and the ship be endangered, a boat would be sent for him. The crew of the *Alaska* arrived in their boats soon afterward and began efforts to recover the vessel's cargo. In the afternoon, Bertholf went ashore and sent a boat to the *Alaska* to pick up Gamble and the seaman.

The wind suddenly shifted and increased, and the sea rose so quickly that the boat was unable to make the wreck and was forced to proceed to the *Bear* instead. As the *Alaska*'s boats left the wreck, Bertholf saw through his glasses that Gamble, the ordinary seaman, and one native man had been left aboard. An additional boat from the *Bear* was unable to approach the wreck. Bertholf, evidently recognizing that if something was not done at once the three people still aboard the *Alaska* would perish, hired three professional surfmen, for a fee of fifty dollars, to go to the wreck through the surf in their dory and bring off the men. After a long struggle, the surfmen reached the wreck, took off the three stranded men, and landed them safely through the surf. Bertholf's quick thinking and decision to employ professional surfmen to rescue the men undoubtedly saved their lives. By the following morning the wreck had been pounded to pieces and the beach was strewn with its wreckage.

This second year of Bertholf's tour as the executive officer of the *Bear* was an especially demanding one. The gold rush had caused a shortage of seamen, and good crewmen were hard to find. The tempers of some of the crew matched the bad weather. Theirs was a demanding life. Shortly after they had arrived back at Unalaska in October, four of the crew were put in the brig for drunkenness. The next day two more were put in the brig and one in single leg irons for being defiant and unruly. Captain Tuttle and Lieutenant Bertholf knew how to run a tight ship, and a tight ship required exercising discipline over the crew. Eventually the captain and his executive officer had to employ ten hands from shore to replace their drunken crewmen in order to carry on ballasting the ship and preparing it for the voyage from Unalaska back to Seattle.

Bertholf was no doubt glad to get back to Seattle when the *Bear* finally moored there on 8 November following a two-week voyage. The gold rush had added many problems to his already long list of duties as the executive officer, but he had been equal to all the demands placed upon him. Not long after returning to Seattle, Bertholf learned that the Department of the Interior needed a Revenue-Cutter Service officer to travel to Russia to arrange for the purchase of a new breed of reindeer to be introduced into Alaska. Here, perhaps, was another challenge to be overcome, another difficult goal to achieve, another adventure. It proved to be one that would take Bertholf literally around the world.

The U.S. government's program to introduce reindeer into Alaska to provide a permanent food supply for the Inuit people began in 1891, when the USRC *Bear* transported the first herd of sixteen reindeer from Siberia to Alaska. Modern hunters with their steam launches and rapid-fire guns had found the whales, walruses, and seals that were the traditional game of the Inuit easy prey. These traditional sources of Inuit food and clothing were fast disappearing. The wild caribou that the Inuit had easily captured before had been frightened away and were increasingly difficult to find. A crisis was developing.

Dr. Sheldon Jackson, the U.S. government's general agent of education in Alaska, saw imported reindeer as a solution to the problem. He arranged for the purchase of the reindeer in Siberia and started the first reindeer colony at Unalaska. Siberian herders were brought in to teach the Inuit how to care for the reindeer. The Siberians were later replaced by Laplanders from northern Norway and Finland who were more skilled in handling and caring for reindeer.

Jackson's Bureau of Education took charge of the deer on their arrival in Alaska and distributed them among government and mission schools, which trained the Inuit people in reindeer culture. Each "graduate" deer man was given the nucleus of a herd. By this deliberate plan, the Inuit were shifted from hunters to herders within a single generation. Although few people realized it at the time, Bertholf and the Revenue-Cutter Service were an integral part of one of the most remarkable social experiments the world has ever seen.

The experiment prospered, and during the succeeding years more reindeer were brought over from Siberia. Eventually there were several thousand in various herds distributed along the Alaskan coast from Point Barrow to Bethel. These reindeer proved invaluable not only for the Inuit people of Alaska, but also in preventing the starvation of the American miners who came to the Yukon Valley during the gold rush and the whalers stranded at Point Barrow in the winter of 1897–98.

The first reindeer brought over from Siberia were from the Chukches herds. By the turn of the century Dr. Jackson and his supervisors at the Department of the Interior had learned of a breed of reindeer much larger, stronger, and sturdier than those they had been purchasing in the neighborhood of the Bering Strait. They set out to try to purchase some reindeer of this Tunguse stock, which were found around the northern end of the Okhotsk Sea.

In the fall of 1900, Bertholf, who was then serving as the executive officer of the USRC *Bear,* wrote to the Department of the Interior expressing his willingness to go to Siberia to purchase some of the Tunguse reindeer. He did not offer his reasons for volunteering for the mission. Perhaps he viewed it as a chance to help the Inuit people, or perhaps he saw it as an opportunity to further distinguish himself in the Revenue-Cutter Service. Certainly such an expedition would present an opportunity to prove himself by overcoming numerous difficulties and challenges. In December 1900 the secretary of the interior requested that 1st Lieutenant Bertholf be assigned to the Department of the Interior for temporary duty in Siberia in connection with procuring the new breed of reindeer.[2]

On 2 January 1901, after returning from thirty days' leave in Englewood, New Jersey, Bertholf was issued orders detaching him from the *Bear* and directing him to report to the secretary of the interior. Upon Bertholf's arrival in Washington, D.C., W. T. Harris, the U.S. commissioner of education, directed him to proceed via Saint Petersburg, Russia, to the region near the Okhotsk Sea where the Tunguse reindeer could be found. Once there, he was to purchase a number of reindeer and have them driven to Admiral Skobolov Harbor in Baroness Korfa Bay on the eastern coast of Siberia. The reindeer would have to reach the harbor no later than 15 May 1901. Bertholf was also appointed a special disbursing agent of the Interior Department with the authority to spend U.S. funds to purchase the reindeer and to pay for the other expenses he would incur on the expedition.

Bertholf departed Washington, D.C., on 11 January 1901 and traveled to New York City, where he boarded the German steamship *Trave* bound for Southampton, England. On the transatlantic voyage Bertholf met a recently divorced young woman named Emilie Inness Sublett. Ellsworth and Emilie spent a great deal of time together before arriving in England.

Bertholf arrived at Southampton on 23 January and then proceeded to Saint Petersburg via Havre and Paris. When he reached the imperial capital on 4 February, Bertholf found himself in the midst of a Russian winter. The average temperature was only 15 degrees Fahrenheit, cold even by Alaskan standards.

The day after Bertholf reached Saint Petersburg he presented himself and his letters of recommendation to Ambassador Charlemagne Tower, who had already been informed by the U.S. State Department of the projected trip. Bertholf knew Ambassador Tower from his lectures on naval history at the Naval War College five years earlier. Bertholf explained the nature of his mission and the necessity for his speedy departure from Saint Petersburg. The winter was already well advanced, and if he did not leave before the end of February, he would have to wait until the following winter to complete his mission.

When no papers had been issued by 18 February, a frustrated Bertholf cabled Commissioner Harris in Washington requesting that the State Department telegraph the U.S. embassy in Saint Petersburg to hasten the paperwork. The ambassador communicated Bertholf's concern to the authorities, and on 20 February the Russian government finally issued the necessary instructions to the various officers of eastern Siberia to facilitate Bertholf's passage and mission. Concerned that it was already too late, Bertholf again cabled Washington with the suggestion that he reach Siberia by sailing to Vladivostock. Washington cabled back that Bertholf should proceed to Irkutsk as ordered.

Departing Saint Petersburg on 24 February, Bertholf reached Moscow the following day and secured an interpreter to accompany him on his mission. Two days later Bertholf and his interpreter boarded a Trans-Siberian Railroad train in Moscow and traveled to Irkutsk, arriving on 8 March. Here, as in every other Russian city or post station that he visited, Bertholf found that every government official he contacted did everything in his power to facilitate the mission.

The rest of his journey would be by sled. With the assistance of the local chief of police, he procured and repaired a second-hand *pavozka,* or covered winter traveling sled, large enough for two persons. The heavy, strongly built wooden sled was long enough for the occupants to lie at full length. The front end contained a seat for the driver as well as protection for the travelers inside the sled. Such sleds were usually drawn by three horses abreast, with one driver. On narrow roads the horses could be harnessed in tandem fashion with an additional driver riding the lead horse. The inside of the *pavozka* was completely lined with thick felt to keep out the wind, and a felt apron could be buttoned to enclose the sled top in case of snowstorms or headwinds. The sled runners were very close together but fitted with an outrigger on each side to prevent the sled from tipping over on uneven roads. The provision box was strapped on the back of the sled. For protection when he was outside the *pavozka,* Bertholf purchased a *shuba,* or greatcoat, of winter deerskins, a pair of deerskin boots, gloves, and a fur cap.

With all preparations completed, Bertholf and his interpreter left Irkutsk on the morning of 13 March. The severest part of the winter was past, and the temperature at Irkutsk varied from 20 degrees Fahrenheit in the day to 2 degrees below zero at night. As they proceeded toward Yakutsk, eighteen hundred miles to the north and reputed to be the coldest part of Siberia, the weather grew colder and colder. During their journey the two men stopped at 122 post stations, located nine to twenty-one miles apart, for fresh horses. Bertholf and his interpreter took turns sleeping in the *pavozka* so that one of them would always be awake to pay for horses at the stations or in case anything untoward happened. Between Irkutsk and Yakutsk there were only two towns of any importance, Kirinsk and Vitim. They reached the former on the fifth day, rested for a day at the small hotel there, then continued on their journey.

The road between Kirinsk and Vitim was extremely rough, and the *pavozka* tipped over twice. The first time was in soft snow and the sled was quickly righted, but the second time everything got soaking wet, including Bertholf, his interpreter, and their drivers. Within a short time their clothes were frozen stiff. When they finally reached Vitim, they remained there long enough to dry out by a roaring fire. The *pavozka* was so badly damaged in the accident that they obtained another one before departing on 22 March.

They pulled into Yakutsk on 28 March, fifteen days after leaving Irkutsk. There Bertholf experienced the lowest temperature of his expedition, 24 degrees below zero. The last leg of the journey, from Yakutsk to Okhotsk, was the most difficult of all. The *pavozka* was too heavy and wide for the road between the two towns, so Bertholf hired a sled builder to construct two single covered sleds and a baggage sled, all of which could be pulled by single horses or by dogs.

When the sleds were completed, Bertholf and his interpreter departed on 6 April, having replenished their stock of provisions and obtained a fresh supply of frozen soup. Because few people in the region between Yakutsk and Okhotsk spoke Russian, the governor at Yakutsk detailed a Cossack who spoke both Russian and Yakut to accompany them. The Cossack rode on the third sled. As the snow deepened and the path narrowed, the horses were replaced by reindeer, and finally by dogs. When they were about halfway to their destination, the caravan ran into a five-day storm, which slowed them down considerably.

As the party neared Okhotsk, Bertholf encountered his first Tunguse deer and saw for himself that this breed was indeed much larger than the breed that had been previously imported to Alaska. On the morning of 19 May, after traveling 750 miles over hilly and thickly wooded land and increasingly difficult roads, the travelers reached Okhotsk. After once more replenishing their supplies, Bertholf and his interpreter headed up the shore of the Okhotsk Sea to Ola, where they arrived on the morning of 29 May. Now that he had finally reached his destination, Bertholf found that purchasing the Tunguse reindeer would not be easy. At first the deer men flatly refused to sell any reindeer at all unless he agreed to take them within thirty days; they would not agree to furnish the reindeer when Bertholf returned with a ship in the spring. After Bertholf offered to pay more for each of the reindeer, however, the two sides reached an agreement. Bertholf also had to procure some eight hundred bags of moss for the reindeer to eat during their trip to Alaska.

His arrangements in Ola complete, Bertholf boarded a steamer and headed south to Vladivostock on 5 July, hoping to charter a vessel to transport the reindeer to Alaska. After calling at the ports of Okhotsk and Ayan, the ship arrived in port on the evening of the sixteenth. Summer was the busy season, and the only vessel Bertholf found available for charter was the Russian steamer *Progress* of Vladivostock. Having met this steamer at Ayan and inspected it there, Bertholf concluded that it was suitable for the limited number of deer that he had been able to obtain. He immediately chartered the *Progress* for three months or less, at a cost of ten thousand rubles a month (about five thousand dollars) in addition to the cost of the coal. For a trip of three months, coal would have to be carried in the cargo space, where Bertholf also planned to put the reindeer, and the owner of the vessel agreed to furnish the lumber to floor over the coal. Bertholf had to purchase the lumber to construct the reindeer's feeding troughs and pens.

After the coal, the stores, and the lumber necessary for flooring and pens had been loaded, the *Progress* departed Vladivostock on 5 August. Before sailing, Bertholf called on the governor of Vladivostock to pay his respects and to receive an order addressed to the local authorities of the northern region instructing them to aid Bertholf as much as possible in his mission. When the *Progress* arrived at Ola on 12 August, there was no time to waste. Summer was nearing its end, and Bertholf hoped to finish the journey before the rough winter weather set in.

The bags of moss were loaded the following day, and over the next seven days 428 reindeer were taken onboard. Bertholf tried to purchase more deer, but the local deer men were unwilling to part with any. Once onboard, the reindeer were distributed among five pens in the hold of the ship. On the afternoon of 20 August the *Progress* left Ola and steamed across the Okhotsk Sea. The weather was rough nearly all the way across, and Bertholf became worried about his precious cargo. The rolling of the ship frightened the deer, which would not lie down until they were exhausted and often trampled the smaller deer; many were injured. Fourteen died on the first day at sea and were thrown overboard. While crossing the Okhotsk Sea they would lose as many as twenty-five reindeer a day.

After rounding the southern tip of Kamchatka they passed through the Kurile Strait, entered the Bering Sea, and headed north. The first two days in the Bering Sea were much smoother sailing, and the deer quieted down. The daily deaths decreased to five. The *Progress* finally reached Port Clarence, Alaska, on 29 August and anchored off the Teller Reindeer Station. The last few days of the voyage had been very hard on the deer, and quite a few more had died. Only 254 of the original 428 reindeer were alive to land at the Teller Reindeer Station. Bertholf had expected to lose some deer on the voyage, but he never anticipated losing such an extraordinary number.

Although the rough weather undoubtedly contributed to the many deaths, Bertholf concluded that four other factors were more important: (1) August–September was the horn-growing season, and the animals were less able to withstand the strain of the rough voyage; (2) the deer were not full-grown; (3) the wooden deck of the reindeer pens on the ship became slippery with the animals' wastes; and (4) the deer had too much room to roam about when they were restless. The Lapp herders at the Teller Reindeer Station disagreed; they attributed the losses mainly to starvation because the feeding troughs were too high off the deck. After unloading the deer, the *Progress* left Port Clarence on 1 September and steamed back to Vladivostock. On the way there the vessel stopped at Ola to land the two Tunguse deer herders who had accompanied the herd, and then proceeded to Ayan. Bertholf arrived back at Vladivostock on 24 September. After terminating the charter of the *Progress* and settling up all accounts connected with the reindeer purchase, Bertholf left Vladivostock on 1 October. He had completed his mission and proved himself once again in the process. From Vladivostock, Bertholf proceeded to California via Nagasaki, Japan, arriving in San Francisco on 6 November. From San Francisco, Bertholf returned by rail to Washington, D.C., to report to the Department of the Interior on his expedition. It is quite probable that Bertholf also filed a classified intelligence report on his observations while traveling across Russia. His arrival at the nation's capital marked the end of the round-the-world trip that had begun the previous January.

In January 1902 officials in the Department of the Interior expressed their "high appreciation for the faithfulness, energy, skill and resources exhibited by him [Bertholf] in performing the very difficult commission with which he had been entrusted."[3] The department also informed the Revenue-Cutter Service that Bertholf's services were no longer needed. The Revenue-Cutter Service granted Bertholf thirty days' leave and sent him home to New Jersey in an "awaiting orders" status.

During this time Bertholf revealed both his genuine concern for the Inuit people and his own character in a letter to the secretary of the treasury dated 11 February 1902. The letter referred to events from the fall of 1899 when Bertholf was serving as the executive officer of *Bear* and had to transport several witnesses to Sitka to testify in court proceedings.

Bertholf explained that he had purchased supplies for them with their witness fees, but when the *Bear* was unable to go north in the spring of 1900, a mix-up had occurred and the supplies had not been sent. Bertholf also noted that he still held the balance of the money belonging to these native witnesses and planned to purchase additional supplies with it and ship them to San Francisco. He requested that the *Bear* transport these supplies to the proper people in the coming summer season. Bertholf ended his letter to the secretary by giving detailed instructions on the delivery of the different lots. He was even aware that one of the witnesses had died, and gave instructions that the supplies he had purchased for her be given to her husband.[4]

Bertholf's expedition across Russia, like his participation in the overland relief expedition in Alaska, demonstrated his willingness to take on arduous missions. Whatever his motivation for volunteering, whether it was to prove his manliness or his dedication to serving his country, or perhaps out of concern for people in need, he had once again distinguished himself by demonstrating initiative, leadership, resourcefulness, and courage in the face of overwhelming obstacles.

~ 6 ~

CLIMBING THE
CAREER LADDER

Having acquired considerable experience as an individual, both during the overland relief expedition and on his recent mission crossing Russia, Bertholf had now reached a point in his career where he needed experience in command if he wanted to continue to progress. Over the next several years Bertholf would serve as the executive officer of a large revenue cutter and as the commanding officer of a small third-class cutter. These assignments would prepare him for the ultimate aim of every seafaring officer—command of a major vessel.

Command of any vessel requires a great deal of technical knowledge of that vessel's machinery and characteristics. It also requires good judgment and the ability to lead men. Life at sea was hard: the men faced poor living conditions, bad food, strict discipline, long absences from home, and demanding and arduous work. It tended to attract only the roughest type of men. Controlling and guiding such men, especially on a ship at sea, takes great skill. Such skill usually comes only with years of experience: as a junior officer, a department head, and then as an executive officer.

In April 1902 Bertholf reported aboard the USRC *Manning*, which was then in a shipyard at Bremerton, Washington. The vessel's previous commanding officer had been detached after bringing the *Manning* into the shipyard, leaving 2d Lt. S. P. Edmonds as the acting commanding officer. Thus when 1st Lieutenant Bertholf reported aboard as executive officer, he relieved Edmonds as the acting commanding officer. The 205-foot *Manning,* the last rigged-for-sail cutter built for the Revenue-Cutter Service, was slightly larger than the *Thetis* and the *Bear.* Built in 1897 as the first of a new class of cutters, the *Manning* had a triple-expansion engine that generated two thousand horsepower and a single screw capable of propelling the ship through the water at more than seventeen knots. The *Manning* was the first cutter to have generators installed to provide lights and bells.

Bertholf got the *Manning* under way on the afternoon of 5 May and headed across Puget Sound on the four-hour trip to Seattle. Two days later Bertholf made the customary official calls on the captains of the *Bear* and the *Thetis,* which were also anchored off Seattle. On 10 May Capt. C. H. McClean reported aboard; he assumed command the following day.[1]

Bertholf assisted his new commanding officer in navigating the *Manning* as it departed Seattle on 15 May and headed out of Puget Sound and up the Georgia Strait to Comox, British Columbia, for coaling. From there, the cutter steamed to the familiar waters off Alaska for what would be Bertholf's third Bering Sea Patrol. It proved to be a routine, uneventful summer, marked only by the usual law enforcement and rescue duties and the conduct of hydrographic surveys. This patrol did provide Bertholf with valuable experience as the executive officer of a large cutter and in navigating the harsh and poorly charted Bering Sea. It was his last Bering Sea Patrol for five years. When Bertholf returned to the area it would be as the captain of his old ship, the *Bear.*

When the *Manning* returned to Port Townsend on 12 November, Bertholf received orders for special duty with the Life-Saving Service. After spending twelve days in Port Townsend, Bertholf headed east, stopping en route to take a few days' leave before reporting to the Life-Saving Service on 19 December 1902. During that leave he married Emilie Innes Sublett, the young divorcée he had met en route to England a year and a half earlier. Herman Vanderwart, the pastor of Bertholf's home church, the First Reformed Church of Hackensack, officiated at the 6 December ceremony.

Bertholf was thirty-six years old on his wedding day, and his bride was twenty-seven. She had a daughter, Dorothy, from her previous marriage.

There was little time for a honeymoon. Thirteen days after the New York City ceremony, the new husband reported for duty with the Life-Saving Service at Atlantic City, New Jersey, as an assistant inspector.

The Life-Saving Service, founded in 1848, was formally organized as a separate agency of the Treasury Department in 1878 and operated under a dual chain of command. Each of its thirteen geographic districts had both a civilian superintendent and an assistant inspector from the Revenue-Cutter Service. The district superintendents reported directly to the general superintendent, also a civilian, whose office was in Washington, D.C. The Revenue-Cutter Service officers assigned to each district as assistant inspectors were in a military chain of command and reported to the inspector of lifesaving stations, a senior Revenue-Cutter Service officer stationed in New York City.

Duty with the Life-Saving Service allowed Bertholf to spend a lot of time with his new wife and stepdaughter, a luxury not always accorded to those in their nation's service. Bertholf was also fortunate to be assigned as the assistant inspector for the Fifth District of the Life-Saving Service, which covered the entire coast of New Jersey. His headquarters was initially at Atlantic City, but since he had the option of locating it anywhere along the coast, he soon moved it to Red Bank, a small city on the Navesink River five miles from the ocean. Only about ten miles south of Sandy Hook, New Jersey, Bertholf's headquarters was about as close to the homes of his mother and his mother-in-law as it could be.

As the assistant inspector, Bertholf made monthly visits to each of the Fifth District's forty-two lifesaving stations, which were located at strategic sites from Sandy Hook in the north to Bay Shore, near Cape May City, in the south. Every lifesaving station was manned by a full-time crew, usually consisting of a keeper and seven surfmen. The lifesaving crews usually executed rescues using surfboats, surfcars, or breeches buoys. At each station, in addition to the ordinary routine of inspection, Bertholf examined and drilled the crews in their duties. On his first tour each year he was accompanied by a physician from the Marine Hospital Service who examined the keepers and surfmen and dismissed any who were physically, mentally, or morally unfit for duty. Whenever a shipwreck in his district involved a loss of life, Bertholf was required to investigate and to determine if the rescue had been properly conducted.

Robert Bennet, a Coast Guard officer who studied the Life-Saving Service, notes that most surfmen and keepers were local residents motivated to do little more than was necessary to keep their jobs. Their lackadaisical work ethic often brought them into conflict with the Revenue-Cutter Service officers who served as assistant inspectors. When they visited the stations, these professional military officers "sought efficiency, conducted inspections, . . . sought to improve the equipment, set up watch requirements, enforced regulations, and in general totally disrupted the *status quo!*"[2] Bennet concedes that sometimes the inspectors were overzealous in dealing with men less well disciplined than those in the Revenue-Cutter Service, but the overall record of the inspectors was one of positive achievement. That is, they kept an important and humane activity operating with more efficiency than might otherwise be expected of personnel who were placeholders interested only in keeping secure jobs.

Independence Day in 1903 was a very sad day for Bertholf. His mother had died the day before while staying with her brother in New York City. Because he was stationed in New Jersey, Bertholf was able to attend the funeral, which was held at the First Reformed Church in Hackensack. Pastor Vanderwart officiated as Mrs. Bertholf's body was laid to rest in the churchyard. Although Annie Francis Bertholf had been the mother of a large family, the obituaries in the local newspapers named only two of her eleven children: her two sons serving in the armed forces, Lt. Ellsworth Bertholf in the Revenue-Cutter Service and his younger brother Wallace, who was an ensign in the U.S. Navy.[3]

August 1904 brought a long-awaited pleasure and honor. Bertholf finally received the special gold medal recommended by President McKinley for his part in the overland relief expedition. The secretary of the treasury, L. M. Shaw, in forwarding the medal, noted that "future seekers for the record of heroic Americans will surely note with pleasure what was done by Lieutenant Jarvis, Lieutenant Bertholf and Surgeon Call within nineteen degrees of the North Pole, in the winter of 1897."[4] The special congressional gold medal of honor, four inches in diameter and one-quarter inch thick, depicts Lieutenant Bertholf's bust on the front with the words, "2nd Lt. E. P. Bertholf, Awarded by Act of Congress—June 28, 1902, For Heroic Service." The reverse side of the gold medal depicts the USRC *Bear* in the background with the three members of the relief expedition in the foreground and the words, "U.S.

Revenue Cutter Bear, Overland Expedition, Relief of Whalers, Nov 27, 1897—Sep 13, 1898." The medal is now in the museum at the U.S. Coast Guard Academy in New London, Connecticut.

The medal would be the most important and best-known honor of Bertholf's career. From that point on, whenever Bertholf was spoken of, the special congressional gold medal of honor would be mentioned as well. Some would even claim later that Bertholf's appointment as commandant of the Revenue-Cutter Service was made "largely because of his heroic, if matter-of-fact dash to Point Barrow."[5]

In October 1904, after almost three years as an assistant inspector, Bertholf's assignment with the Life-Saving Service came to an end and he was ordered to report to the USRC *Onondaga* at Philadelphia. His tour of duty with the Life-Saving Service would prove especially valuable ten years later when he oversaw the merger of that service with the Revenue-Cutter Service to form the U.S. Coast Guard.

Bertholf reported aboard the *Onondaga* on 16 November for his third tour of duty as an executive officer. His wife did not accompany him to Philadelphia, evidently preferring to remain near her mother in northern New Jersey; or perhaps she did not want to move her daughter to a new school. In any event, they remained at Red Bank during Bertholf's next two duty assignments on the East Coast. Bertholf became a "geographic bachelor" for the next several years as he commanded ships homeported first in Philadelphia and later in Wilmington, North Carolina.

The cutter *Onondaga* patrolled the Atlantic coast from Cape Hatteras north to Great Egg Harbor searching for vessels in distress and for derelicts that might pose a hazard to ships at sea. In November 1906, after serving one year as the *Onondaga*'s executive officer, Bertholf was detached from that vessel. On 9 November Bertholf reported to the USRC *Wissahickon* in Philadelphia and proudly assumed his first command. The *Wissahickon* was a two-year-old, ninety-six-foot harbor tug with a complement of eleven men. Although small, the vessel would test his aptitude as a commander and his fitness for advancement and for command of larger cutters.[6]

The *Wissahickon* patrolled Philadelphia harbor to enforce all anchorage laws and port regulations. The captain of every vessel entering the harbor was given a map of the harbor by the harbormaster indicating where the vessel could and could not anchor. When Bertholf discovered a ship anchored outside the proper anchorage, it was his duty to order the captain to move the vessel. If the ship did not move under its own power, the *Wissahickon* or a private tugboat would tow it. Large sailing vessels often required assistance in moving to their assigned anchorage. Bertholf's command was probably not a very exciting duty, but it was necessary to prevent collisions and shipwrecks within the harbor. Philadelphia was a major international seaport, and Bertholf, although a relatively junior officer, had to deal with both American and foreign captains with tact, good judgment, and firmness. Occasionally there were more interesting missions than the *Wissahickon*'s usual harbor patrols. One such time was in April 1907 when Bertholf conducted a harbor tour for a congressional committee responsible for legislation dealing with ports and waterways.

On 7 June Bertholf encountered every ship captain's worst fear. While the *Wissahickon* was working alongside the Norwegian steamer *Drot* there was a misunderstanding concerning the bell signals from the *Drot*'s pilothouse and the *Wissahickon*'s bow struck the *Drot* a slight blow on the starboard side, forward of amidships. Bertholf, his chief engineer, and the first mate of the *Drot* examined the site and found no damage beyond some scraped paint. The mate of the *Drot* declined Bertholf's offer to repaint the scraped surface. Bertholf considered himself lucky that no greater damage had been done. Fortunately, that was the only mishap of note that occurred while Bertholf was in command of the *Wissahickon*.

About nine months into his command, Bertholf left the *Wissahickon* for a week to appear before a board in Washington, D.C., to be examined for promotion to captain. His chief engineer became the acting commander during his absence. Bertholf returned to the *Wissahickon* on 30 July and was notified two weeks later, on 13 August, that he had passed the written and physical examinations. He took the oath of office and received his commission as a captain in the Revenue-Cutter Service on 31 August 1907. Soon thereafter he received orders to report to the *Seminole* for duty as temporary commanding officer. On 20 September Bertholf was detached from the *Wissahickon*, again leaving his chief engineer as the acting commanding officer.

The very next day, Captain Bertholf reported aboard the USRC *Seminole* in Wilmington, North Carolina, read his orders to the assembled crew, and assumed temporary command during the short absence of Capt. J. H. Quinan, who had been detached for special duty.[7] Built in

1900, the *Seminole* was somewhat smaller and had a lighter draft than the *Onondaga;* it carried a complement of eight officers and fifty-nine enlisted men. While it would be a very short tour of duty, his temporary command of the *Seminole* would give Captain Bertholf some opportunity to put into practice the knowledge of multiship maneuvers he had learned at the Naval War College.

On 12 October Captain Bertholf received orders to take the *Seminole* from Wilmington to Fishermans Island in Chesapeake Bay for drills with a Revenue-Cutter Service fleet. He was to arrive by the sixteenth and report to the senior officer commanding the fleet for inspection and joint drills. Revenue cutters generally acted independently, but their experience with the navy during the Spanish-American War had pointed out the need for training and experience in operating as a part of a squadron or fleet. Bertholf got the *Seminole* under way on 13 October and proceeded up the coast and into Chesapeake Bay, where he anchored off New Point Comfort three days later.

The following day Bertholf paid an official call on Capt. W. E. Reynolds, the fleet commander. As the superintendent of the School of Instruction, Captain Reynolds had been designated the senior officer of the exercise. Little did either man realize that four years later Bertholf would take precedence over Reynolds as the captain-commandant of the Revenue-Cutter Service, and that twelve years after that Bertholf would recommend Captain Reynolds to succeed him as commandant of the Coast Guard.

The vessels of the exercise fleet included the *Apache, Algonquin, Forward, Onondaga, Seminole,* and *Pamlico.* The fleet exercise began on Sunday, 20 October. At the signal of the flagship, the *Algonquin,* Bertholf got the *Seminole* under way and with the other cutters formed a single column that proceeded up the York River and anchored off Yorktown. On Monday, each cutter landed a fully equipped landing force on the signal of the flagship. On Wednesday, all the vessels got under way again, and Bertholf again brought the *Seminole* into column with the other cutters. About an hour later the vessels formed two columns. Following target practice that afternoon, all the vessels returned to anchor off Yorktown.

After completing more drills, Bertholf took the *Seminole* to Newport News, Virginia, arriving on the thirtieth. Captain Quinan, after a little over a month away, relieved Captain Bertholf and retook command of the *Seminole* on 1 November.

One can only speculate how pleased Bertholf must have been to receive orders to proceed on 14 November to assume command of the USRC *Bear* in Oakland, California. The *Bear,* on which he had served twice before, was the most famous cutter in the nation, and to be selected as its commanding officer was an honor certain to benefit one's career. Bertholf returned home to Red Bank, New Jersey, to prepare his wife and stepdaughter for the move to Oakland. It would prove to be an exciting and demanding tour of duty—and it would also be Bertholf's last assignment afloat.

⚜ 7 ⚜

COMMAND AT SEA

*W*hen Captain Bertholf and his family arrived in San Francisco in the fall of 1907, three-fourths of the city was still in ruins from the earthquake that had destroyed it less than two years earlier. Much of the population was still living in tent cities. An epidemic of bubonic plague made the situation in the city even worse. Fortunately, the Bertholfs chose to make their home across the bay in Oakland, at 953 Madison Street.

The *Bear* was undergoing repairs at the Mare Island Naval Shipyard on San Pablo Bay, across the Napa River from Vallejo, when Bertholf arrived. Despite the heavy forward construction of the *Bear*'s frame and all the measures taken by its builders to produce a staunch ship, the vessel required periodic overhaul. No ship ever built can withstand the wear and tear of the sea and the wind forever. Threats came from beneath the waves as well. Marine organisms that bored into the *Bear*'s wooden planking weakened the ship's structural integrity. The *Bear* had been at the Mare Island yard since 1905 for a major overhaul that included many modernizations. A flying bridge had been constructed on top of the pilothouse with a small brass steering wheel connected to the wheel in the pilothouse. Wireless communications, electric lights, and other changes brought the ship up-to-date and made it better able to deal with the difficulties of Bering Sea duty.[1]

On 19 December the *Bear* was placed back in commission and Bertholf relieved his former commanding officer, Capt. Francis Tuttle, who was completing his third and final tour of duty in the ship. Chief Petty Officer Judson Thurber, the boatswain, presided over the *Bear's* enlisted men. Thurber had served on the *Bear* since the days of Capt. "Hell Roaring Mike" Healy and would continue to run things in the forecastle throughout Bertholf's command. A great sailor who came from a long line of New England fishermen, Thurber was also said to be one of the most skilled users of profanity ever to tread a forecastle. In his history of the *Bear*, Frank W. Wead alleges that on one occasion, when a green hand received an order to "check a hawser and held it fast instead of easing it away as required, causing the line to part, Thurber emitted a string of twenty-seven epithets without repeating himself or drawing a breath."[2]

Bertholf now filled the position every seagoing officer yearns for: commanding officer of a major ship. Joseph Conrad gave perhaps the best description ever written of the commanding officer on a navy ship. His words apply equally to the captain of a revenue cutter, and "Revenue-Cutter Service" could be exchanged for "Navy" in the following quotation with no loss of accuracy.

Only a seaman realizes to what great extent an entire ship reflects the personality and ability of one individual, her Commanding Officer. To a landsman, this is not understandable, and sometimes it is difficult for us to comprehend, but it is so!

A ship at sea is a distant world in herself, and in consideration of the protracted and distant operations of the fleet units the Navy must place great power, responsibility, and trust in the hands of those leaders chosen for command.

In each ship there is one man who, in the hours of emergency or peril at sea, can turn to no other man. There is one who alone, is ultimately responsible for the safe navigation, engineering performance, accurate gunfire and morale of the ship. He is the Commanding Officer. He is the ship!

This is the most difficult and demanding job in the Navy. There is not an instant during his tour as Commanding Officer that he can escape the grasp of command responsibility. His privileges in view of his obligations are almost ludicrously small; nevertheless, Command is the spur which has given the Navy its great leaders.

It is a duty which most richly deserves the highest, time-honored title of the seafaring world—CAPTAIN.

On Christmas Eve, Captain Bertholf guided the *Bear* away from the shipyard and then on to its normal anchorage off Sausalito on the Marin Peninsula, north across the bay from San Francisco. The following spring he took the *Bear* to various shipyards in San Francisco and Oakland for additional repairs before the next summer's Bering Sea Patrol.

On 1 May 1908 Captain Bertholf received orders to assist in the reception of the U.S. Navy's Atlantic Fleet during its upcoming visit to San Francisco. This force of sixteen first-line battleships was known as the Grand Fleet or the Battle Fleet. Because they were painted white, as every American warship had been since the appearance of the metal navy in the 1880s, later generations would refer to them as the "Great White Fleet." It would be the job of the *Bear,* along with the *Manning* and the *Alert,* to maintain a clear path through San Francisco Bay when the fleet arrived on 6 May.

The previous December President Theodore Roosevelt had sent the Great White Fleet, under the command of Adm. Robley D. "Fighting Bob" Evans, on a 14,400-mile journey to the West Coast. After leaving Magdalena Bay in Lower California, Mexico, the fleet, now under the temporary command of Rear Adm. Charles M. Thomas (Evans's deputy) because Evans was in poor health, divided into four squadrons. Each squadron visited a different California port prior to sailing on to a tumultuous welcome in San Francisco. Admiral Thomas would unexpectedly and suddenly die while the fleet was in San Francisco, and Rear Adm. Charles S. Sperry would lead the fleet on to Puget Sound for refitting and back to San Francisco to coal for the cruise that Roosevelt announced would continue to the Far East. But that was still in the future as Bertholf made his preparations to greet the fleet.

The city was in a high state of excitement as the big day approached. In April 1908, weeks before the Great White Fleet was scheduled to arrive in San Francisco, local school and city officials prepared for the event by declaring 6 May a holiday. Businesses, with the exception of banks, and schools would be closed so that the entire citizenry could celebrate the occasion.

On 6 May all of San Francisco and visitors from elsewhere in the West, a million people in all, turned out to greet the battleships. Prior to the fleet's arrival, pleasure craft filled with onlookers sailed around the fourteen ships of the Pacific Squadron, which had arrived on 4 May and were at anchor off Angel Island. The USS *Yorktown,* a small cruiser that served as the squadron's flagship, carried Secretary of the Navy Victor M. Metcalf to greet the fleet.

After sailing around the anchored ships of the Pacific Squadron, most of the excursion boats then sailed past Sausalito on their way to the quiet waters off Baker Beach, on the west side of the Presidio, which was generally believed to be the best place to watch the arrival of the battleships and their escorts. In February the *New York Times* had anticipated that the gathering of the two fleets would be the "greatest naval spectacle ever known in the Pacific."[3] Forty-six ships, together with at least a score of smaller auxiliaries, would make up what the *Times* called "the greatest review in the history of the American Navy."[4]

Admiral Evans, who had left the fleet on 14 March for treatment and recuperation in California, rejoined the Great White Fleet for the climactic pageant at San Francisco. His flagship, the *Connecticut,* drifted in the fog off the Golden Gate as a parade of forty-two warships formed behind it. In addition to the escort ships that accompanied the fleet, every gunboat and torpedo boat on the California coast had come to San Francisco to join the procession. Precisely at noon on 6 May the fog lifted, revealing the seemingly endless column coming through the Narrows.[5]

The *Bear* took station off Fort Point on the south side of the Golden Gate. When the *Connecticut,* with Admiral Evans in the emergency cabin on the after-bridge, reached the Golden Gate, it was greeted by hundreds of excursion craft of all descriptions. There were stately passenger steamers, lumbering coastal schooners, spotless white steam yachts, graceful sailing craft from the clubs at Sausalito, and swarms of little gasoline launches. It must have appeared to Captain Bertholf as if anyone who could beg or borrow a ride on something afloat had taken to the water to see the battleships, with their gleaming hulls and dazzling figureheads, close at hand.

After the last vessel of the fleet had passed Fort Point, Bertholf ordered one blank shot to be fired from the *Bear*'s gun, as dictated by the special rules for the marine parade. When the last vessel was a quarter mile past Fort Point, the *Bear* fired two more blank shots, again as dictated by the special rules. The *Bear* then followed behind the fleet, keeping the excursion vessels from crowding the last ships in the line.

Previously published regulations ordered all pleasure vessels to keep clear of the fleet as it entered, and for the most part the sightseers obeyed the rules. Captain Bertholf dealt with those who did not. Only a few minor infractions occurred. Whenever a boat tried to force its way too close to the fleet's path, Captain Bertholf ordered a short blast on the *Bear*'s steam whistle to let the skipper of the guilty boat know he was venturing into forbidden waters. That was usually enough to stop the incursion. The biggest offender was the large passenger steamer *Whittier*, which ignored the *Bear*'s whistle and cut into the path of the fleet. Captain Bertholf gave chase at that point and ordered his forward 6-pounder to fire a shot well across the intruder's bow. The skipper of the *Whittier* obeyed this second warning and returned to the sidelines.[6] Small sailing vessels and gasoline launches darted here and there, hoping to escape notice because they were small and therefore inconsequential. But no boat was too small for Captain Bertholf's vigilant eye. His assignment was to keep the course clear, and he was not overlooking anybody.

When the last ship of the grand parade had passed Alcatraz and anchored off San Francisco, Bertholf's work was finished. The *Bear*, the *Manning*, and the *Alert* gave all the civilians on the water permission to inspect the battleships and cruisers at closer range. The revenue cutters still had to do some policing because some of the small launches insisted on getting too close to the anchored ships. By the end of the day, Captain Bertholf could take satisfaction and pride from the fact that there were no accidents among the hundreds of boats crisscrossing the bay that day.

Bertholf had played an important role in an occasion unique in the history of the western United States. The governors of half a dozen western states came to San Francisco to welcome the battleships of the U.S. Navy, and thousands of citizens from surrounding states had come along with them. Railroad officials estimated that more than 300,000 visitors traveled to San Francisco during the forty-eight hours preceding the fleet's arrival.[7]

A few weeks after the visit of the Grand Fleet the *Bear* prepared to get under way for its first Bering Sea Patrol under Bertholf's command. Four revenue cutters were to make up the Bering Sea Patrol Fleet for the summer of 1908. Captain Bertholf would be the ranking officer of all the vessels and would be serving under Senior Capt. F. M. Munger, the fleet commander.[8]

The sealing controversy that had brought the revenue cutters to the Arctic in the first place remained unresolved. Although the fur seal industry had brought nine million dollars into the U.S. government treasury to date, two million more than had been paid for Alaska, the government seemed unable to protect its most lucrative possession from foreign poachers. During the summer of 1908 the Japanese would be the primary offenders.

Preserving the seals from extinction was a national concern. Americans objected to pelagic sealing—killing seals, especially female seals, while they were swimming or resting in deep water. The British were prohibited by treaty from killing seals at any time within a zone of sixty miles surrounding the Pribilof Islands. The Japanese, however, were bound by no such treaty and were rapidly exterminating the seal herd by hunting in waters outside the three-mile limit.[9]

To prevent the loss of this national resource, the Revenue-Cutter Service, which had served as the representative of the United States in Alaska since its purchase from Russia, patrolled the sealing grounds of the North Pacific and Bering Sea to enforce the sealing agreements then in force. The national importance of this situation is evident in the assignment of several revenue cutters and even a U.S. Navy light cruiser to the patrol.

The coming summer promised to produce an abundance of poachers. The end of the Russo-Japanese War had released Russia's warships to patrol their own sealing grounds, which severely curtailed the Japanese raids there.[10] Furthermore, the Japanese government had doubled the subsidy it paid for seal skins, which greatly encouraged both the number and the audacity of seal poachers, who now moved east to raid American rookeries. Often they went in close to shore and fired shots to scare the seals out beyond the three-mile limit where they could be killed legally. At other times the poachers lurked behind a fogbank and stole onto the beaches, killing the seals there. These raids had become so serious that the Treasury Department had assigned four revenue cutters to the Bering Sea Patrol for the 1908 season and the Navy Department had assigned the USS *Yorktown*.

On 17 May the *Bear* left San Francisco at 9:00 A.M. and proceeded north, following the general coastline at a distance varying from fifteen to twenty miles. The men of the *Bear* enjoyed good weather during the passage to Sitka and saw neither sealing vessels nor seals. After anchoring off Sitka on 24 May, Bertholf went ashore to call on the collector of customs and the U.S. marshal to investigate the report of Japanese schooners marauding around the islands near Sitka. Their information that no sealing vessels had been seen in the vicinity of Sitka for some time coincided with his own judgment that any sealers remaining in the North Pacific had probably moved westward.

After replenishing his ship's water supply, Bertholf sailed out of Sitka on the evening of the twenty-fifth. The *Bear* had hardly passed out of the Eastern Channel when Bertholf's chief engineer reported that the main condenser was leaking and the boiler was taking in salt water rapidly. Aware that the auxiliary condenser was not sufficient for the cruising needs of the vessel, Bertholf decided to return to an anchorage at Sitka where the boiler could be blown down and the condenser overhauled. Revenue cutters had to be self-sufficient in remote areas such as Alaskan waters; there were no shipyards or support facilities available. The cutter crews were responsible for all repairs that might be needed. When all the leaks in the condenser had been found and repaired, the *Bear* lifted anchor on 27 May and again steamed northward.

Bertholf decided to sail first for Kodiak Island and then westward along the south side of the Alaska Peninsula. Neither sealing vessels nor seals were seen in these waters either, and good weather prevailed until 1 June, when an easterly gale forced the *Bear* to anchor for the night. The gale abated the next morning, and Bertholf set his course for Unalaska. Upon arriving there, however, thick fog forced the *Bear* to delay and stand off until the third, when the fog lifted enough for the *Bear* to pass through and anchor at Unalaska.

After conferring with the commander of the Bering Sea Patrol, who had his headquarters at Unalaska, the *Bear* departed on 8 June to patrol around the Pribilof Islands. Eleven days later, off Black Point, the officer of the deck on the *Bear*'s bridge sighted a schooner headed west across the northern tip of Saint Paul Island. The schooner, under sail alone, was making very little headway, and the *Bear* managed to close with it. At 10:00 A.M. Captain Bertholf sent one of his officers aboard the schooner to look for evidence of illegal sealing. When none was found, Bertholf allowed the vessel to depart.

Captain Bertholf then took his ship to Village Cove on Saint Paul Island and anchored in mid-afternoon. A message from the agent onshore informed Bertholf that the lookout on Northeast Point had seen two Japanese boats sealing within one mile of the point. Aware that the cutter *McCulloch* was in sight of the point, Bertholf decided to keep the *Bear* at anchor and let the other cutter deal with the sealers.

While the *Bear* was at Saint Paul Island, Captain Bertholf gave his crew a two-day leave "with their money in their jeans." He was proud that every man came back clean, sober, and on time. In spite of the rigid discipline that Bertholf maintained on his ship, there was not one desertion. Under Bertholf's command the *Bear* had overcome its reputation as the "boozing Bear."[11] Bertholf had developed a respect for discipline since his days as a rebellious cadet that would serve him well throughout the remainder of his career.

Early on the morning of 21 June, with the *Bear* still lying at anchor off Saint Paul Island, Bertholf and his crew heard a number of shotgun reports nearby, but no one could see through the patchy fog to determine their source. At 5:10 A.M. the *Bear* got under way and started steaming in the direction of the gunfire. A few minutes later the fog lifted and Bertholf could see a schooner bearing north by northeast of him. Shortly thereafter he saw a rowboat on the starboard bow rowing rapidly in the direction of the schooner. Bertholf steamed alongside the rowboat for a look. The boat contained a crew of three Japanese with guns, ammunition, and provisions, together with one fresh female seal skin and one unskinned seal, also a female and not quite dead. The boat belonged to the *Saikai Maru* of Hakodate, Japan. Bertholf placed the three crewmen in custody aboard the *Bear* and took their boat in tow while he steamed toward the schooner the boat had been heading for.

By this time the fog had cleared enough for Bertholf to see several schooners in various directions, as well as many small boats offshore and inshore of them. The sounds of shooting continued. Bertholf determined at a glance that only two of the schooners were sealing illegally, and he was already heading for one of them. By this time the latter schooner had made all sail and was attempting to move offshore in haste. The other boats in view soon began returning to their respective ships. At about 6:00 A.M. Bertholf brought the *Bear* alongside the schooner and found that it was indeed the *Saikai Maru* of Hakodate, whose boat he had just seized.

Since the schooner was inside the prohibited sealing zone of the island and some of its boats were even further inshore, and since at least one of those boats carried freshly killed seals, Captain Bertholf seized the *Saikai Maru*. He sent Lieutenant Alexander and three armed crewmen onboard the Japanese schooner to keep it from escaping while the *Bear* investigated the other illegal sealing vessel.

That schooner was now also under all sail, towing several of its boats behind it, but making very little headway in the light air. On closer examination the schooner proved to be masquerading as something it was not. The vessel's original rig had been changed to that of a topsail schooner, and its hull had been painted white and a fake smokestack added, so that from a distance it looked like the revenue cutters *Rush* and *Perry*. Bertholf blew several blasts of the *Bear*'s steam whistle as a signal to heave to, but the sealer paid no attention. Bertholf then ordered a blank shot fired from the forward gun, whereupon the schooner called in its boats and hauled down its sails. At 6:23 A.M. Bertholf edged the *Bear* alongside this schooner and found it to be the *No. 2 Kinsei Maru* of Tokyo. Captain Bertholf sent Lieutenant Hinckly and a boarding party to inspect the vessel. No seal skins or carcasses were found, but there was fresh blood in several of the boats. Because it was inside the prohibited sealing zone of the island and several of its boats showed signs that they had been sealing, Bertholf seized this vessel too and left one of his warrant officers and three armed crewmen aboard as a prize crew.

With the *Kinsei Maru* in tow, Bertholf steamed back to the *Saikai Maru* and took it in tow as well. After towing both schooners to Village Cove and anchoring, Bertholf sent two of his officers aboard each vessel to count the seal skins and examine the ships' papers. The papers and all the weapons that were found were brought back aboard the *Bear*. The three Japanese crewmen aboard the small boat that Bertholf had seized were confined for the night aboard the *Bear*.

That evening the *Rush* returned from a trip to Saint George and anchored near the *Bear* at Village Cove. Captain Bertholf arranged for the commanding officer of the *Rush* to take the two seized schooners and all the papers, persons, and articles connected with the seizure to Unalaska and deliver them to the commander of the Bering Sea Patrol Fleet. Since the complement of the *Rush* was small, Bertholf detailed two of his officers and two of his crewmen as a prize crew for the *Kinsai Maru*. His role in the affair did not end there, however. The two Japanese sealing vessels would take up a good deal of his time over the next two months.

The *Bear* resumed patrolling the Pribilof Islands, but on 1 August Bertholf received orders to transport the masters and crews of the two seized Japanese sealing schooners to Unga for a hearing. The *Bear* left the next day, taking the inside passage to Unga and arriving on the evening of the fifth. The U.S. commissioner came onboard at Unga and arranged to hear the cases against the two Japanese schooners the following day.

After hearing the charges against the *Kinsai Maru*, the commissioner referred the case to the grand jury at Valdez. The next day the commissioner conducted a hearing on the case against the *Saikai Maru* with the same result. Captain Bertholf and his officers, who were witnesses in the cases, were also bound over by the commissioner to appear before the grand jury at Valdez on 1 October. On the afternoon of 7 August, Captain Bertholf turned the masters and crews of the two Japanese schooners, together with their effects, over to the U.S. marshal at Unga ashore, then took the *Bear* to Sanborn Harbor to investigate reports of violations of the sealing laws there.

Before long, however, the Bering Sea Patrol Fleet commander ordered Bertholf to pick up the Japanese prisoners at Unga and take them to Valdez, and to remain there for the grand jury hearing and the trial. The *Bear* arrived at Unga on 15 September but was leaking badly and could not sail on to Valdez until the twentieth. In addition to the fifty-nine Japanese prisoners charged with illegal sealing, Bertholf also had to transport a prisoner charged with rape, a detained witness, two guards, and a deputy U.S. marshal. In all, he had to accommodate sixty-four passengers aboard the *Bear* on the voyage to Valdez. On the way the *Bear* stopped at Seward on 24 September, where another deputy U.S. marshal turned over a crew member from the revenue cutter *McCulloch* who was to be taken to San Francisco for trial by court-martial.

Knowing that they would be in Valdez for some time during the grand jury hearings and trial, Bertholf turned over the latter prisoner to the custody of the U.S. marshal at Valdez for safekeeping until the *Bear* was ready to head south. The grand jury indicted the Japanese shipmasters and their crews for illegal sealing on 20 October. The trial was delayed until 2 November in order to obtain an interpreter. By 6 November both masters and their crews had been convicted. Since Bertholf did not have to return the masters and crews to their seized vessels in Unalaska, he sailed from Valdez on the tenth after taking back aboard the prisoner he had received at Seward. After a brief stop to take on coal at Sitka on 13 November, the *Bear* proceeded south to San Francisco.

Captain Bertholf brought his ship safely back through the Golden Gate and to anchor at its homeport of Sausalito on 2 December. The *Bear* would winter there, undergoing crew training, overhaul, and preparation for the next season's Bering Sea Patrol.

Shortly after the *Bear* arrived back at Sausalito, the commandant of the Revenue-Cutter Service, Captain-Commandant Worth G. Ross, announced his intention to retire three years hence in May 1911. Bertholf, aware that just a few months earlier Congress had granted the commandant of the Revenue-Cutter Service the same rank and pay as a captain in the U.S. Navy, decided to compete for the position. High-level positions were rare in the Revenue-Cutter Service. In addition to Ross's singular rank and position, six billets had been established in 1908 for the new rank of "senior captain." These positions provided the first opportunity in the history of the Revenue-Cutter Service to advance commissioned officers beyond the rank of captain, a rank equivalent to a U.S. Navy lieutenant commander in grade, although at less pay. Ross's impending retirement set off a competition among at least fourteen officers who sought to replace him. Bertholf would be among them.[12]

On 22 January 1909 Bertholf mailed a confidential letter to his good friend and fellow Revenue-Cutter Service officer Capt. Godfrey L. Carden about the upcoming vacancy. Carden, himself a former naval cadet at Annapolis, had been an underclassmen on the fateful cruise of the USS *Constellation* during the summer of 1883. He had resigned from the Naval Academy in October 1885 and gained an appointment to the Revenue-Cutter Service after Bertholf did. The two men had thus been fellow cadets first at the Naval Academy and later at the Revenue-Cutter Service School of Instruction. They had kept in touch in the years since and were good friends. Even though Carden was an underclassman at the School of Instruction while Bertholf was an upperclassman, he had been commissioned a third lieutenant year one earlier than Bertholf, who was held back by his disciplinary problems, and was thus senior in rank.

In the letter, Bertholf asked Carden if he was planning to make a run to succeed Ross as the next commandant. Bertholf conceded that he would like to have the job himself but would gladly stand aside if Carden wanted it because he thought that Carden would make an even better commandant than he would. Carden could probably get the necessary backing if he chose to run, Bertholf told him, and he assured Carden of his own support if he chose to pursue the position. If, however, Carden did not want the job, Bertholf wanted to know so he could make his own plans to run, and he wanted Carden's support. Bertholf also shared his plans not to make a "service campaign" as Ross had done. His efforts to gain the post would be entirely outside the service.[13]

Bertholf did not receive a reply to his letter until late March. Carden had been transferred to Belgium and Bertholf's letter had been delayed in transit. In his response, Carden did not commit himself to support Bertholf, but he did suggest that Bertholf go ahead with his campaign. Carden wished Bertholf success in anything he decided to undertake and agreed with him that help for his selection must come from outside, not inside, the service.[14]

That same March, the secretary of the treasury announced that the *Bear,* the *Manning,* the *Perry,* and the *Rush* would compose the Bering Sea Patrol for the upcoming summer. The *Thetis* was designated to make the annual cruise to the Arctic. On 7 May Bertholf was directed to take onboard six cases and two crates, together with 250 gallons of gasoline in five iron containers, and to transport them to Unalaska for delivery to the fur-seal agents on the Pribilof Islands.

Bertholf ordered up-anchor on 4 June, steamed the *Bear* out through the Golden Gate, and headed northward. The cutter reached Sitka on the night of the fifteenth, paused for two days, then continued on patrol. On 23 June Bertholf sent boarding parties aboard three Canadian seal schooners northeast of Chirikof Island. They had all sailed from Victoria, British Columbia, and since no evidence of illegal otter or seal hunting was found, they were allowed to proceed.

The 1909 patrol season would prove much less eventful than that of the previous year. Bertholf and the *Bear* were assigned to patrol the territorial waters on the north and east sides of Saint Paul Island. By the middle of July they had sighted only two schooners. That same month, word arrived from the commander of the Bering Sea Patrol Fleet that at the end of that season the *Bear's* new homeport would be San Diego rather than Sausalito.

The *Bear* left Unalaska on 18 July with Capt. W. V. E. Jacobs, commander of the Bering Sea Fleet, as a passenger. Jacobs wanted to consult with the chief government agent at Saint Paul Island concerning the maintenance of an efficient patrol. Bertholf dropped Jacobs at Village Cove on the night of the twentieth and then proceeded with the *Bear* to his assigned patrol station northeast of Saint Paul Island. These waters had been the most frequented by the sealing fleet in the 1908 season, but this summer the sealers had kept almost exclusively southwest of the island. The *Bear* boarded only two Japanese sealing schooners, both outside U.S. territorial waters. On 6 August Bertholf decided to look for poachers in the waters around the Pribilofs, but according to the ship's log, the weather was "so boisterous that there have been but two or three days during which pelagic sealing could be carried on."[15]

In early September the *Bear* transported six Japanese sealers who had been seized on Walrus Island by the Saint Paul Island seal agent to Unalaska. Departing on the eleventh, Captain Bertholf turned the *Bear* westward, taking the Bureau of Education agent and a surgeon to investigate conditions at the villages of Atka, Nikolski, and Chernokski. On the nineteenth the *Bear* left Chernokski harbor and proceeded back to Unalaska, arriving that evening.

That fall Bertholf would find himself involved in yet another Alaska rescue mission. This one, however, proved much less dramatic or newsworthy than the overland relief expedition of 1897–98. In early October he was directed to proceed to Nome, to confer there with Judge A. S. Moore, and then to transport about one hundred destitute men and women to Seattle. The fleet commander chose the *Bear* for this assignment because its duty for the season was nearing an end and it had sufficient space and carried enough rations to accommodate and feed so many extra people. To ready the ship for the voyage, Bertholf purchased the materials needed to construct extra bunks to accommodate the unexpected passengers.[16]

The *Bear* arrived at Nome on 9 October and departed that same night with 143 destitute people onboard; among them were three men who were quite ill. Since the *Bear* was without a sick bay, Bertholf transferred two of the sick men to the *Manning* when the *Bear* arrived at Unalaska on the thirteenth, and the third was sent to the *Thetis* for transportation to Seattle. After coaling, the *Bear* sailed for Seattle on the fourteenth with the remaining passengers.

Captain Bertholf guided his ship into Seattle on 1 November, discharged his passengers, then steamed to Ladysmith, where he took on coal before proceeding to San Francisco. Captain Jacobs, the fleet commander, released the *Bear* from the Bering Sea Patrol Fleet and included a commendation for Captain Bertholf in the release order:

> It affords me pleasure to say that I have always found your command ready for the work at hand, that the arduous and constant patrol duty about the Pribilof Islands and in the sixty-mile zone has been performed with discretion and zeal, and that good judgment and careful attention to detail have marked your dealings with situations that have called for decisive action.[17]

After reaching its new homeport of San Diego on 14 November, the *Bear* was ordered to cruise from the Mexican border to San Pedro, California, during the winter. The very next month, however, Captain Bertholf found himself back in much more familiar waters when he was directed to take the *Bear* back to San Francisco and to be at the Mare Island Navy Yard by 23 January. The *Bear* rounded Point Loma and headed north on 20 January 1910, arriving at its familiar Sausalito anchorage two days later and at Mare Island on its scheduled day of the twenty-third. The ship, with a leaking stern tube, would undergo repairs and overhaul throughout the remainder of the winter.

On 2 May 1910 Captain Bertholf conned his ship through the Golden Gate and headed north for his last Bering Sea Patrol. As Bertholf had more than likely hoped, his final cruise as the commanding officer of the *Bear* would be an Arctic trip to Point Barrow, where Bertholf had gained fame as an Arctic hero thirteen years earlier. It would be the *Bear*'s first cruise to Point Barrow in four years.

The ubiquitous fog always made the passage through the Bering Sea and Arctic Ocean difficult. It blinded watch officers and lookouts, and made even well-known waters seem strange and unfamiliar. As the *Bear* was running before an easterly gale through Unimak Pass toward the deeper, safer waters of the Bering Sea, it ran into just such a blanketing fog. Unimak Island, astern, was the last bearing the ship had taken. Aware of the strong and unpredictable currents flowing through the pass, Bertholf, who knew these waters well, laid a course well to the north of any possible land lying ahead. When the lookout at the cathead suddenly called down that there was land dead ahead, Bertholf ordered the helm hard aport. The crew raced to their sail stations, and the *Bear* swung up into the wind and slowed, pitching in the head seas. Close-hauled on a starboard tack, the *Bear* took up a new course, still in the enshrouding fog. Changing course under sail power, or tacking, was much more difficult than making a sudden turn when steaming under power. Tacking involved shifting the sails from one side of the boat to the other, and the crew had to come on deck and loosen some lines and haul on others to shift the sails. The maneuver involved coordinated action by the entire crew. Fortunately, the new course was a safe course, and the *Bear* sailed unscathed through Unimak Pass.

The *Bear* reached Nome on 14 June and after a brief stay sailed on north to Point Barrow. The summer and early autumn passed without noteworthy incident, and at the conclusion of the season's patrolling the *Bear* turned southward, arriving in Seattle on 3 November. From there it headed home to San Diego, arriving there on 6 December. Captain Bertholf was detached a few weeks later, leaving his executive officer, 1st Lieutenant Wheeler, as the acting commanding officer.

Bertholf's tour as commanding officer of the *Bear* had added luster to his good reputation. He had demonstrated good judgment in both law enforcement and humanitarian situations. He had guided his ship through the always hazardous and frequently stormy waters of the North Pacific, the Bering Sea, and even into Arctic waters on his voyage to Point Barrow. Bertholf had handled his crew with firm discipline but also with fairness, as evidenced by their reenlistment for another cruise. It was a tour of duty that would serve him well in his future career and especially in his quest to become the commandant of the Revenue-Cutter Service.

Bertholf's last ship would be the iron-hulled USRC *Morrill.* The *Morrill,* considerably smaller than the *Bear,* normally cruised the Great Lakes. During Bertholf's brief tour of duty as its commander, however, the vessel was laid up for the winter at Detroit. Without the day-to-day demands of commanding a vessel at sea, Bertholf had time to press his campaign to succeed Ross as the next commandant.

He had stiff competition for the post. Oscar Hamlet, the most senior officer of the service after Ross, was not eligible because he would reach the mandatory retirement age in a few months. Hamlet, however, endorsed Senior Capt. William E. Reynolds as the "best equipped" for the position. Captain-Commandant Ross had recommended Senior Capt. John C. Cantwell as his successor.[18] Cantwell, an 1882 graduate of the Revenue-Cutter School of Instruction, had a distinguished record of accomplishment at sea, in both the Atlantic and Pacific Oceans. However, and fortunately for Bertholf, Cantwell's record was not perfect. As commanding officer of the *McCulloch* in 1905 he had taken his wife and some friends on a short trip from California to Oregon without getting prior permission from headquarters to have guests onboard. He had also failed to record their presence in the ship's log. In addition, two years later he had run the *Manning* aground in Prince William Sound. Although an investigation cleared him of any liability, Cantwell had again failed to record the events accurately in the log. The official reprimands Cantwell received for his poor judgment in both situations undoubtedly hindered him in his campaign to become commandant.[19]

Bertholf was acutely aware of his own imperfect record, of course. After all, he had been dismissed from the Naval Academy for his involvement in a hazing incident aboard the USS *Constellation*. Of perhaps greater concern was the fact that he stood considerably lower in seniority on the lineal list of officers than Cantwell. Cantwell was a senior captain and third on the list of seniority, while Bertholf was only a captain who stood twenty-third on the list.

Bertholf also had some important assets. Congress had unanimously awarded him a gold medal for his role in the overland relief expedition of 1897–98; he had commanded several vessels, most recently the venerable *Bear*; and he had served successfully on a number of Bering Sea Patrols. In addition, Bertholf was willing, and able, to use political influence from outside the service to get the job, while Cantwell apparently was not. Bertholf must have been aware that Article 658 of the Revenue-Cutter Service Regulations forbade him to use "political or other influence" to gain a position, but just as surely he knew that such influence had been used before, even if not to obtain the highest office in the service.

Fortunately for Bertholf, Walter E. Clark, governor of the Alaska Territory, was in Washington in early April. At a gathering that included Secretary of the Treasury Franklin MacVeagh, Clark took the opportunity to endorse Bertholf as Ross's successor. MacVeagh asked him to put his recommendation in writing, which Clark did later in the week. Clark noted that he had known Bertholf for fifteen years and wrote of their "warm friendship." He was not endorsing him out of friendship, Clark wrote, but rather on account of Bertholf's personal and professional qualities. He was "a man of much originality and executive ability—a man who does his own thinking and has intelligent ideas for the improvement of the Revenue-Cutter Service." The governor also noted his long association with the Revenue-Cutter Service and both the importance of the service to Alaska and of the territory in the affairs of the service. These circumstances, Clark wrote, prompted his interest in the impending appointment.[20] Clark's endorsement proved invaluable to Bertholf's campaign. Clark was a personal friend of the Taft family and a frequent visitor to the president's summer home. Other candidates for the appointment had their supporters as well, of course, but none was as influential as Governor Clark.

Bertholf wrote to Secretary MacVeagh conveying his desire and qualifications to be the next commandant. After Captain-Commandant Worth Ross retired on 30 April as he had planned, MacVeagh forwarded Bertholf's name to the president as his recommended successor. President Taft sent Bertholf's name to the Senate for confirmation as the new commandant on 22 May.

The Senate, however, delayed his confirmation. The public health surgeon and navy officers who had been nominated for promotion at the same time as Bertholf were confirmed three days later, on 25 May. The army promotions and a professor of chemistry at the U.S. Military Academy, also nominated the same day as Bertholf, were confirmed on 6 June while Bertholf was still waiting to hear.

Perhaps the senators delayed the confirmation because they wanted to know why a relatively junior captain had been selected over twenty-two officers senior to him. The senators were perhaps also interested in the fact that Bertholf had been dismissed from the Naval Academy after one year—and indeed, had the 1907 regulations been in effect in 1885, Bertholf could not have been admitted to the School of Instruction.

On the other hand, Bertholf had received the congressional gold medal, had attended the Naval War College, had dealt with the Russian government and traveled across Russia, and had proven himself as a commanding officer. All in all, Bertholf's record must have been convincing because on Friday, 15 June, the Senate finally confirmed him to succeed Worth Ross as the captain-commandant of the Revenue-Cutter Service. Subsequent events would confirm MacVeagh's good judgment in choosing Bertholf.

~8~

COMMANDANT, U.S.
REVENUE-CUTTER SERVICE

Early in June, Bertholf and his wife and stepdaughter moved into a house at 1643 Harvard Street in the District of Columbia. Their new home was located just a few blocks north of the Capitol and not far from the Revenue-Cutter Service Headquarters offices. Bertholf's office was on the leased fourth floor of the Munsey Building, on the northwest corner of 14th and E Streets in the northwestern sector of the District of Columbia, Room 419. On Monday, 19 June 1911, Bertholf took the oath of office as captain-commandant of the Revenue-Cutter Service, succeeding Worth G. Ross, who had retired the previous April. The title "captain-commandant" was, at the time, both a title and a rank. On taking the oath of office Bertholf not only became the commandant of the Revenue-Cutter Service, he also was promoted two ranks: from captain—skipping the rank of senior captain—to captain-commandant, the only rank in the Revenue-Cutter Service equivalent to a U.S. Navy captain.

Serving as commandant was an entirely new experience for Bertholf. As a Revenue-Cutter Service officer in the field he had worked primarily with the service's personnel, either senior officers or the crews of his ships. As the commandant he would function in an entirely new arena; he would have to work with politicians and bureaucrats, most of whom knew little, if anything, about the Revenue-Cutter Service. The new post would require political sensitivity and tact in dealing with all sorts of individuals.

For a time, it seemed that Bertholf's first year as commandant might be the Revenue-Cutter Service's last. Under Bertholf's direction, the service underwent major organizational changes as it fought for its institutional survival. In 1911, at the same time Bertholf took over as commandant, the increasing complexities of administering the service led the Treasury Department to divide the Revenue-Cutter Service Headquarters staff into six divisions: operations, engineering, construction, ordnance, supply, and law. A Revenue-Cutter Service captain was assigned to head each division and to advise and assist Bertholf in these specialties. In the field, operational and administrative control of cutters was finally stripped from customs collectors and vested in service officers. The following year, 1912, Bertholf established two Revenue-Cutter Service divisions (districts) on each coast, with headquarters at San Francisco and Port Townsend, Washington, on the Pacific coast, and at New York and Boston on the Atlantic coast. Gradually, the division commanders assumed operational control over the cutters within their districts. Cutters operating outside those divisions—for example, on the Gulf of Mexico coast and in Alaskan waters—were responsible directly to the commandant. Bertholf became the first commandant to serve in a military chain of command in the Revenue-Cutter Service, and he could control all the cutters through his division commanders.

Early in July 1911, just a month after becoming commandant, Bertholf addressed a problem he had experienced as an assistant inspector with the Life-Saving Service. Revenue-Cutter Service officers detailed as assistant inspectors were supposed to be under the supervision of the inspector, a senior Revenue-Cutter Service officer stationed in New York City. Because this officer also held the post of superintendent of construction for the Life-Saving Service, he was an inspector in name only. In reality, the general superintendent of the Life-Saving Service in Washington, D.C., a civilian, supervised and directed the assistant inspectors. Bertholf had experienced this situation firsthand as a first lieutenant when he had served as the assistant inspector for the Life-Saving Service in New Jersey. Bertholf's suggested solution to the problem was a recommendation to the assistant secretary of the treasury that the inspector be relieved of his responsibilities as superintendent of construction so that he could give his entire time and attention to the work of directing and supervising the assistant inspectors in the field. The assistant secretary approved Bertholf's recommendation.

Bertholf, who had spent much of his career in the Bering Sea protecting fur seals, was undoubtedly interested when representatives from Great Britain, Russia, Japan, and the United States finally came together in Washington, D.C., on 7 July to sign a much-needed treaty for the "Protection of Fur Seals and Sea Otters." The treaty was to go into effect on 15 December 1911 and was to continue in force for a period of fifteen years. The Pribilof Islands were declared a sanctuary for the seals, and the United States agreed to stop leasing the islands to private interests. The pursuit, capture, or killing of fur seals in the Pacific Ocean north of the thirtieth parallel was declared unlawful, and severe penalties were established for poachers. The Seas of Japan, Kamchatka, Bering, and Okhotsk were included in the prohibited area. Only native Aleuts, Inuits, and other aborigines living along the American and Canadian coasts would be permitted to carry on limited pelagic sealing, and this only in canoes or undecked boats propelled by paddles, sails, or oars. No firearms were permitted, and no primitive boat was to carry more than five hunters.[1]

In January 1912 the House Committee on Foreign Affairs held hearings on implementing this treaty at which Bertholf was asked to testify. Bertholf told the committee that the treaty would be a great step forward because it included four nations that conducted large-scale sealing operations instead of just the United States and Britain, as the former treaty had. He concluded his testimony with an impassioned description of the perils faced by the Revenue-Cutter Service in Alaskan waters.

> This patrolling of the waters surrounding the Pribilofs is one of the most severe duties which befalls any branch of the public service. The weather conditions are uniformly bad, and a dense pall of fog surrounds the islands for about half the time during the months of July and August. There are no lights nor fog signals in these waters, and the only warnings of the near approach to the land are the roar of the breakers and the bellowing of the seals in the rookeries. As fog conditions are naturally the best for making raids, the worry and anxiety of the officers in charge of the cutters can well be imagined.
>
> There are no harbors in which to seek shelter, so that from 15 to 20 days at a time the cutters must continually cruise about, the monotony

being varied only by the occasional visits to the headquarters at Unalaska, 225 miles away, for coal, water, and other supplies. To the credit of the service it can be stated that notwithstanding the dangers of these surroundings, there has been but one vessel lost in the 40 and more years in which revenue cutters have cruised Alaskan waters. . . . The enforcement of the treaty conditions on the part of the United States will require the service of every available revenue cutter on the Pacific coast from the time that the seals start northward in the spring until they return in the fall, as it must not be supposed, with such valuable prizes at stake, that the existence of this treaty will prevent lawless men from making the attempt to capture seals both on land and at sea. The value of any law depends on the rigidity with which it is enforced, and I can only say that with its record of the past as a guide for the future the Revenue-Cutter Service will be able to cope with the situation, and thus, so far as the United States Government is concerned, at least the intent of the treaty will be carried out to the letter.[2]

The House of Representatives passed an act implementing the treaty on 24 August. Among other things, the implementation act directed the president "to cause a guard or patrol to be maintained in the waters frequented by the seal herd or herds and sea otters, in the protection of which the United States is especially interested, composed of naval or other public vessels of the United States designated by him for such service."[3]

Only revenue cutters would carry out the patrols. The Bering Sea Patrol Force was the group designated by the president to maintain the seal patrol. For the purposes of the convention, the cutters became a de facto international maritime police force backed by the authority of four major powers.

The convention brought an abrupt end to pelagic sealing and gave the seals a new lease on life. By 1914 the Bering Sea Patrol Force commander was able to report to Bertholf that the area was entirely clear of marauding vessels throughout the season and that the size of the Pribilof Islands herd had noticeably increased. Bertholf believed, however, that pelagic sealing would resume if the patrols stopped.[4]

While the challenges in the Bering Sea were decreasing, Bertholf and the service were facing new challenges in home waters. Passage of the Motor Boat Act of 9 June 1910 gave the Revenue-Cutter Service jurisdiction over motorboats sixty-five feet or shorter in length. The service would now be boarding and inspecting the growing number of pleasure boats to ensure that they carried minimal safety equipment (lights, life-jackets, fire extinguishers, etc.).[5]

One issue, however, dominated Bertholf's tenure as captain-commandant. Less than six months after assuming his post, Bertholf found himself fighting for the very survival of the Revenue-Cutter Service. On 17 November 1911 Frederick A. Cleveland, President Taft's chief economic adviser, presented Congress with the report of the Commission on Economy and Efficiency, a six-man commission chaired by Cleveland that soon became known as the Cleveland Commission. The commission had conducted a detailed study of the federal machinery and of the business practices employed by various government departments.

The Cleveland Commission's report on the Revenue-Cutter Service broke with the suggestions of earlier groups that had recommended moving the service into the navy. After what it described as careful study, the commission concluded that "the service has not a single duty or function that cannot be performed by some other existing service, and be performed by the latter at much smaller expense on its part." Therefore, the commission recommended abolishing the Revenue-Cutter Service altogether and distributing its duties and equipment among other existing branches of the government.[6] The Revenue-Cutter Service's deep-sea "marine-police" duties—as the commission labeled offshore distress work, derelict destruction, and one or two other nonmilitary functions—would be assigned to the navy; its other duties would be assigned to several existing civil maritime agencies. The commission made no recommendation about reassigning Revenue-Cutter Service personnel, leaving that issue to be resolved after a decision was made on the other recommendations. The commission calculated that these changes would result in savings of one million dollars per year—40 percent of the service's annual budget. In other words, after 121 years of service to the nation, the Revenue-Cutter Service was to be eliminated.[7]

Congress distributed the commission's report to the Treasury Department, the Navy Department, and the Department of Commerce and Labor for comment. Charles Nagel, the secretary of commerce and labor, responded with arguments for and against the proposed changes. Secretary of the Navy George von L. Meyer gave Congress a plain statement of what his service's attitude must always be: "Although the chief functions of the Revenue-Cutter Service can be performed by the Navy, this cannot be done in the regular performance of [the navy's] military duties. All duties which interfere with the training of the Navy's personnel for war are irregular and in a degree detrimental to the efficiency of the fleet."[8] Not only did the navy not want the Revenue-Cutter Service's nonmilitary duties, it did not want its personnel, either. Having recently overcome personnel problems of its own, the navy did not wish to face the questions about pay, precedence, and privilege that were certain to arise if it had to absorb the three hundred officers and cadets and the 1,390 enlisted men of the Revenue-Cutter Service. Meyer emphasized that if the navy had to take over the revenue cutters' jobs, it would need both the revenue cutters and the enlisted personnel who operated them—but it did not want the officer corps. The ratio of officers to enlisted men in the navy was one to sixteen; in the Revenue-Cutter Service it was one to four.

Secretary of the Treasury MacVeagh, like Bertholf, was astonished by the commission's recommendations, which, he said, "came out of a clear sky." MacVeagh, of course, was aware of past proposals to transfer the service into the navy. But he probably thought that such a transfer, if effected, would give the Revenue-Cutter Service a status similar to that of the Marine Corps. No one had ever before suggested abolishing it. In a letter to President Taft, MacVeagh expressed his amazement that the Cleveland Commission's recommendation to eliminate the Revenue-Cutter Service had come "at a time when the Service was performing such conspicuous and heroic work, and when its fit equipment and its high usefulness were in immediate and conspicuous evidence. . . . To abolish a service with such a record and such present significance would be unprecedented."[9]

MacVeagh also forwarded a seventeen-page memorandum from Bertholf to the president. The memorandum contained an impassioned plea for the life of the Revenue-Cutter Service, but it focused on economic considerations, which had been the Cleveland Commission's main concern. Bertholf included a survey of the service's duties and addressed the question of the organization's efficiency, then evaluated the commission's assertion that distributing the duties and equipment of the Revenue-Cutter Service would save money and increase efficiency.

Bertholf and the commission agreed on what the various duties of the Revenue-Cutter Service were. But Bertholf argued that the commission members had failed to appreciate the need for an armed patrol to prevent smuggling. "It is true," he contended, that

> this form of lawlessness—smuggling in bulk—is not common, but this fact is direct evidence of the high state of efficiency in which the Revenue-Cutter Service has been and is being maintained, and is the result of the accumulated deterrent effect of years of vigilant patrol . . . and it is clear that without an armed coast-patrol smuggling would soon spring into existence along our many miles of sea-coast.[10]

Bertholf cited figures to demonstrate that the nation received more value from the services of the cutters than it cost to operate them, and that the service had become more efficient with the passage of time. There would be no savings, he insisted, if the government abolished the Revenue-Cutter Service and distributed its vessels to the navy and civil departments to perform work presently being done by the cutters.

Bertholf had public support on his side as well. The commission's report caught the public's attention, and no newspaper, commercial organization, or individual outside of the commission members and the president voiced approval for its recommendations. This response by the press and the public was encouraging to Bertholf as he fought to save the service. An editorial in *Outlook* magazine, for example, questioned the wisdom of the Cleveland Commission and presciently suggested that all vessels that did not belong to the Navy Department might be combined under "what could be called a coast guard service" with the Revenue-Cutter Service at the head of "this combined coast service." The editorial went on to laud the Revenue-Cutter Service's "splendid record of good work done," including "scores of instances of romance, adventure and daring."[11] Chambers of commerce in several maritime cities sent resolutions to the Senate protesting the proposed abolition of the Revenue-Cutter Service. The resolutions were printed in the *Congressional Record* and referred to the Committee on Commerce.[12]

President Taft weighed the Cleveland Commission's report against the reports from the many opponents of the commission's recommendations and decided in favor of his economic adviser. On 4 April 1912 he recommended that Congress enact legislation to implement the commission's recommendations. Taft argued that the country had in effect been maintaining two navies and using one of them (the Revenue-

Cutter Service) to perform duties of a civil character. He therefore recommended that the Revenue-Cutter Service be abolished.

Secretary of the Treasury MacVeagh, convinced of the wrongness of
the commission's recommendations, decided to take another tack. He
ordered Bertholf to work with Sumner Kimball, the head of the Life-Saving Service, to draft a bill to unite the Revenue-Cutter Service and the
Life-Saving Service. Bertholf and the seventy-eight-year-old Kimball set
to work and came up with a bill to create the Coast Guard.

Bertholf's efforts to save the Revenue-Cutter Service were helped by
coincidental circumstances that he had no way of foreseeing. Only a few
days after Congress had received President Taft's recommendation, a
burning ship and a thrilling rescue burst into the newspaper headlines.
The circumstances were made to order to demonstrate the value of both
the Revenue-Cutter Service and the Life-Saving Service as well as the
advantage of merging the two. The *Ontario,* carrying thirty-one passengers and a crew of fifty, also carried a flammable cargo of cotton, resin,
and turpentine. After midnight on 8 April, in a heavy sea off the Long
Island coast near Montauk Point, a fire broke out in the forward hold
and spread rapidly, erupting through the deck in roars as turpentine bar-
rels exploded. In an effort to save his passengers and crew, the captain of
the *Ontario* turned the ship toward the beach. At 3:00 A.M. the keel ran
aground outside the breakers, where at least the vessel could not sink.
Wireless still had the glamour of a scientific miracle at that time, and the
newspapers made much of the heroism of the *Ontario*'s operator, a
teenager named Herbert Ingalls, whose radio distress calls brought the
cutters *Mohawk* and *Acushnet* to the scene. Meanwhile, the beach patrol
of the Ditch Plains Life-Saving Station had spotted the blazing ship. The
surfmen were already at sea in their boat when the liner grounded. Soon
all the passengers and part of the crew had been brought ashore. When
the rising surf became too dangerous for boats, the *Acushnet* kept watch
close to seaward, its own boats ready in the water to rescue those
remaining on the *Ontario* if needed.[13]

The captain and crew remained aboard the *Ontario* for hours trying
to put out the fires. When the fire finally forced the men to abandon
ship, some were picked up by the cutters while others rode a high-line
breeches buoy that the surfmen had rigged earlier. Not a life was lost.
No one had even been injured. An editorial in the *New York Times* called
it "a wreck to be proud of."[14] The cooperation between the rescuers at

sea aboard the cutters and the lifesavers on the shore illustrated the complementary roles of the two services and lent support to Bertholf's and Kimball's proposal to merge the two.

Within a week of the *Ontario*'s rescue another disaster at sea reinforced the importance of well-organized marine rescue agencies. On 14 April 1912 Bertholf was undoubtedly horror-struck along with the rest of the nation to learn that the White Star liner RMS *Titanic,* on its maiden voyage from England to the United States, had collided with an iceberg and sunk at latitude 41 degrees, 46 minutes north, longitude 50 degrees, 14 minutes west. The sinking took the lives of 1,517 people; 711 others survived in partly filled lifeboats and rafts. The *Titanic* disaster, while it occurred far beyond American waters, added a note of great solemnity to the merger debate.

Icebergs had for many years been the dread of transatlantic sailors, particularly those who traveled the sealanes near the Grand Banks of Newfoundland. In the days of slow steamers, most vessels took a course directly across the Grand Banks, which carried them through the ice zone during a large portion of the year. The faster ships of today follow routes established well to the south of the normal ice zone. Unfortunately, the limits of the ice fields and icebergs varied considerably in location as well as in season. Before 1912 nothing had been done to establish any system for guarding against the danger from floating ice along the transatlantic steamship lanes. The *Titanic* tragedy called forth an almost universal demand for a patrol of the ice zone to warn passing vessels of the limits of danger from day to day during the season.

In response to this demand, the Department of the Navy detailed the scout cruisers *Birmingham* and *Chester* to take turns patrolling the regions of the North Atlantic susceptible to icebergs for the remainder of the season. The scout ships were instructed to locate all icebergs in the danger zone and to broadcast daily radiograms alerting all vessels in the area to their presence. They also sent this information daily to the Navy Hydrographic Office, which made it public for the benefit of the maritime world. With this information, the Hydrographic Office could move the steamship lanes southward as the ice danger developed. The two navy vessels maintained the patrol from 19 May to 6 July of that year.

Bertholf believed that revenue cutters were better suited for ice patrols than the larger navy vessels because their operational costs were less. Coast Guard historian Irving King has suggested that Bertholf also wanted cutters to take on the ice patrol at least partly to increase the public's awareness of the service, thus perhaps enabling it to fight off the attack by the Cleveland Commission.[15]

Bertholf suggested to the Treasury Department in early January that the Revenue-Cutter Service could maintain the patrol at considerably less expense than the navy. He pointed out that the service did not need a special vessel to do this work, noting that the *Bear* performed the same duty in the Bering Sea each spring. Bertholf suggested that the *Seneca* and *Miami* be detailed for ice patrol in the Atlantic. During the absence of these two cutters from their stations, the other cutters along the coast could temporarily expand their operating ranges to maintain a constant patrol along the coast.[16]

Secretary MacVeagh agreed that the Revenue-Cutter Service could more appropriately perform this service but questioned his authority to assign it. He also expressed concern that taking the *Seneca* and *Miami* away for five months might spread the service too thin. He feared that "it would look as though we had a surplusage [sic] now if we could afford to detach our two newest and best vessels for nearly half the year."[17]

Bertholf responded to MacVeagh's concern about authority by arguing that the purpose of the ice patrol would be to safeguard and protect life and property at sea, one of the particular duties of the Revenue-Cutter Service. In response to MacVeagh's other concerns Bertholf pointed out that during the late spring and summer months when the icebergs became a menace, good weather usually prevailed on the Atlantic coast and the cutters were able to relax somewhat from their constant and strenuous winter work. Bertholf concluded his memorandum to MacVeagh by summing up his philosophy about the Revenue-Cutter Service.

> As you well pointed out, we might be spreading out rather thin, and it is possible that the navigation laws, motor-boat laws, etc., would not be as rigidly enforced during the three months that the two vessels were absent from the coast, but in making my memorandum I took the view that the safeguarding of life and property at sea through the ice patrol was a duty that should be done by the Revenue-Cutter Service, even at the risk of temporarily slighting some of the other duties of the Service. It may be that in my desire to have the Service assume this duty, which seems to be one of its particular functions, I am proposing something that may over-

tax our complement, but our training forms the habit of endeavoring to accomplish whatever is to be done with the tools that are given us, and our experiences teach us that a task is often less difficult in retrospection than in contemplation.[18]

The Navy Department had intended to continue its ice patrol each year, but on 28 February 1913 the secretary of the navy officially notified the secretary of the treasury that it would have to abandon the ice patrol for that year. Determined to protect American lives during the continuing Mexican civil war, the U.S. Navy kept many of its ships on gunboat duty off Mexican ports during this time. Unsettled conditions in West Indian waters likewise indicated a potential need for the ships originally intended for the ice patrol.[19]

Two weeks later, Franklin MacVeagh and the rest of the Taft administration left office. Bertholf now had to win over a new secretary of the treasury, William G. McAdoo. He drew support from the Maritime Association of the Port of New York, whose members sent a letter dated 13 March 1913 to Secretary McAdoo requesting that he assign revenue cutters to ice patrol duty.[20] Bertholf used the association's request as an opportunity to recommend to McAdoo that two cutters be detailed to patrol the ice danger zone.[21] On 29 March the secretary agreed that Revenue-Cutter Service ships should establish a patrol of the ice fields during the coming season. Pleased with the decision, Bertholf assigned the *Seneca* and *Miami* to this duty. Based in Halifax, Nova Scotia, they would alternate on duty in the danger area.

The Revenue-Cutter Service's first ice patrol, a rugged business, brought the service new renown. No vessels were sunk or damaged by collision with icebergs that year, and the timely warnings provided by the cutters' daily broadcasts were praised by mariners and shipping executives alike. Copies of the ice patrol reports were in considerable demand and furnished material for articles published in the *New York Times, Scientific American,* and *Popular Mechanics* within the next few months.[22] Addressing the secretary of the treasury in a letter dated 8 July 1913, the president of the New York Maritime Exchange declared:

> The knowledge that the [*Seneca* and *Miami*] were alternately stationed in the ice fields, with facilities for furnishing to vessels on the trans-Atlantic route prompt and full information by wireless of ice, weather conditions,

etc., not only created a feeling of security on the part of travelers, but was most reassuring to all interested . . . in trans-Atlantic traffic. . . . That the United States Government had at its disposal two such serviceable vessels, officered by men especially fitted and qualified for this important duty, is a source of great gratification. . . . We believe the success of this patrol during the past season has been so marked as to justify its continuance each year, and we would therefore respectfully recommend that this special duty be made a permanent function of the Revenue-Cutter Service.[23]

Jules Jusserand, the French ambassador to the United States, relayed congratulations to the Revenue-Cutter Service from an officer of the French navy:

The value of the patrol conducted by the United States Revenue-Cutter Service during the year 1913 is beyond appreciation. Their devotion, endurance and intelligence probably saved many lives, and their observations will make it possible hereafter to adopt safer tracks than heretofore. . . . One of the cutters warned me long in advance of the presence of several icebergs directly on the international road of the sea.[24]

So widespread was the anxiety about icebergs that an international maritime conference was scheduled to convene in London in the fall of 1913 to discuss safety at sea. Congress passed a resolution on 28 June 1912 providing for American representation at the conference. A joint meeting of the Senate Committee on Commerce and the House Committee on the Merchant Marine and Fisheries (having jurisdiction over legislation concerning merchant vessels and their navigation, crews, etc.) agreed on 3 January 1913 that the United States should be represented at the conference. On 7 April the secretary of commerce advised the secretary of the treasury that he would like the representatives to be Revenue-Cutter Service officers, saying that he knew "of no more experienced and competent authority on the subject than E. P. Bertholf, Captain-Commandant of the Revenue-Cutter Service."[25] Bertholf was thus among the twelve men appointed on 1 October to represent the United States at the International Conference on the Safety of Life at Sea, which was to convene in London on 12 November 1913. On 28 October Bertholf sailed from New York, bound for London, aboard the SS *Oscar II*.

Bertholf was among the ninety-six accredited delegates from seventeen nations who met in plenary session at the Foreign Office in London on the morning of 12 November 1913. At a second plenary session held the next day, six committees were appointed to focus on different aspects of maritime safety. Bertholf was among the twenty-nine delegates appointed to the Committee on Safety of Navigation. The other American appointed to the committee was Capt. George F. Cooper, the U.S. Navy Hydrographer. The committee met for the first of nine sessions on 14 November. Sir Normal Hill of Great Britain chaired the meetings, at which each nation had one vote. Bertholf obviously took a leading part in the committee's deliberations; its report recognized the work of the Revenue-Cutter Service and recommended that the United States continue the ice patrol.

In addition, Bertholf attended the sixteen meetings of the American delegation in London at which the important propositions before committees were discussed and where ample opportunity was afforded each delegate to express his opinions. After full discussion, the delegation then voted on the position the United States would take as a nation. Other national delegations held similar meetings. Bertholf got a short break from committee work when the conference was suspended from 20 December to 4 January for the Christmas holidays.

The conference met again in plenary session on 19 January 1914 and unanimously adopted the convention in its completed form. All the delegates signed it on 20 January, bringing to a close the seventy-day conference. The International Convention for the Safety of Life at Sea provided for the establishment of an International Ice Observation and Ice Patrol to be directed by the United States, which had borne the entire cost of the patrol the previous two years. It requested the United States to assume the duty of an annual ice patrol on the basis of contributions by the maritime powers. The United States was asked to contribute $30,000 of the projected cost of $200,000; the other nations would provide the remaining $170,000. The delegates to the conference considered the ice patrol so useful that they urged its establishment during 1914 and 1915, in advance of the convention's official enforcement date of 1 July 1915. Bertholf must have been proud when the convention noted that the members of the conference were "united in approving the work which the United States has already done . . . and there was no dissent from the general wish for its continuation and a general desire to contribute to the expense."[26]

Bertholf and the other U.S. delegates arrived back in New York City on 29 January 1914. A week later, on 7 February 1914, President Woodrow Wilson directed the Revenue-Cutter Service to undertake the ice patrol. Bertholf ordered the *Seneca* and *Miami* to initiate the first International Ice Patrol. At the end of the 1914 season, Ambassador Jusserand placed the international community's stamp of approval on the patrol by stating that "the services which the government of the United States intended to render . . . are fully as effective as expected and are such as to call for the sincere gratefulness of the mariners of all countries."[27]

Bertholf could take great satisfaction that the Revenue-Cutter Service's popularity at home had spread abroad. When the Senate Committee on Foreign Relations held hearings about the newly signed International Convention for the Safety of Life at Sea, Bertholf was among those called to testify. Responding to specific questions about the manning of boats as specified by the convention, Bertholf spoke from his personal experience:

> Now, about the certificates of these boatmen, the best lifeboat man in the world is not of any use ordinarily on [a] ship until he has been trained in teamwork. It is teamwork that gets the boat away from the ship. I have seen many boats lowered in very rough weather, and they were always under the supervision of an officer. They did not leave it to the best man on the ship to lower the boat; he knows how to lower it, we hope, because he has been taught, but that officer tells him when to lower and how to lower that boat.[28]

Some senators felt that lifeboat men ought to be qualified seamen trained in rough weather to lower boats. Bertholf testified that he did not think such a requirement either feasible or necessary. Improperly trained boatmen were not a safety problem, he insisted. Supplementing what Capt. George F. Cooper had said earlier to the committee, Bertholf offered his own opinion on the reasons for the *Titanic* disaster, all of which the convention under consideration addressed:

> There are two rules of this convention which if they had been in force at the time of the *Titanic* disaster would have prevented this disaster. The first rule is that if ice is reported on or near the track the master must go at moderate speed, or he must leave that portion of the ocean. Had the

Titanic . . . departed from that portion of the ocean, she would not have hit the iceberg. If she had been running at moderate speed and still have hit the iceberg she would not have damaged herself to so great an extent as to have sunk so soon.

There is still another [important rule]. This prescribes a constant wireless watch, . . . under that regulation, all of the passenger ships going across the Atlantic would have to maintain a constant watch, and the unfortunate condition of the *California* would not have obtained. The man would have heard the signal of distress when he was almost within sight of the *Titanic*. . . . You will recall that when the *Titanic* struck the iceberg the wireless operator on the *California* had gone to bed. The captain did not tell him to get up again to listen. So he did not know anything about the catastrophe until the next morning, when it was too late. She was only 10 or 15 miles from that ship. Furthermore, another rule to which I call attention is the fact that the captain of the *California* and his officers seemed to think that those signals from the *Titanic* were not distress signals, because at that time and the present time you can use distress signals for other purposes.[29]

Convinced of its utility, the Senate ratified the treaty. The service had a new duty: the International Ice Patrol. When the navy bowed out of the patrol after one season and the Revenue-Cutter Service took it over, few voices were left to argue that the cutters' duties should be given to the navy.

Congress had not acted on the Taft administration's recommendation to abolish the Revenue-Cutter Service before Taft left office; nor had it acted on the Treasury Department's alternative proposal to combine the Revenue-Cutter Service with the Life-Saving Service. On 12 April 1915, a little more than a month after President Wilson and his administration took office, Senator Charles E. Townsend of Michigan introduced a bill (S. 760) to create the Coast Guard by combining the Life-Saving Service with the Revenue-Cutter Service.[30] On 26 May 1913 he reintroduced the bill with a few minor changes as S. 2337.[31] President Wilson's extensive legislative program caused further delay, and the bill had to vie for attention with other important legislation for almost two years. Throughout these trying months, while Bertholf was watching the status of the bill, he never said whether he supported it or merely considered it preferable to the dissolution of the service. While he was waiting for Congress to decide the service's fate, he continued with his administrative duties.

Bertholf's predecessor, Captain-Commandant Ross, had prevailed upon Congress to transfer Fort Trumbull, at New London, Connecticut, from the War Department to the Treasury Department to serve as a home for the service's School of Instruction,[32] and the school had moved to Fort Trumbull on 15 September 1910. Although the Fort Trumbull facilities left much to be desired, they were a vast improvement over the facility at Arundel Cove, Maryland, the school's first shore facility, built in 1900. Bertholf had pleaded with Congress from the time of his appointment as captain-commandant to increase the number of cadets in order to meet the service's need for officers. While the Cleveland Commission's recommendation to abolish the Revenue-Cutter Service was under discussion, however, a clause was slipped into the Civil Sundry Bill of 1913 barring the appointment of any additional cadets without specific permission from Congress.[33] It appeared to Bertholf that the dismantling process was already beginning. By 1914 there were only five cadets at Fort Trumbull. There were ten vacancies at the School of Instruction that could not be filled. Bertholf appealed to Congress for relief.

When Congress provided for the appointment of seven cadets during 1913, Bertholf appealed for an additional seven. The following year Congress increased the number to fourteen. The same year, 1914, Bertholf appointed Capt. Frederick C. Billard superintendent of the school. Billard continued to adjust the course of instruction, now of three years' duration, to keep pace with the current needs of the service and to raise cadet standards generally. At the same time, Bertholf announced that henceforth the School of Instruction would be named the "Revenue-Cutter Academy," a term he considered "much more in consonance with the standing of this institution for the education of the cadets."[34]

Bertholf also fought for the welfare of the service's enlisted force. Many of its members were aliens who had difficulty obtaining naturalization papers. The naval appropriations act of 30 June 1914 provided that any alien who had served an enlistment of not less than four years in the U.S. Navy or Marine Corps and had been honorably discharged would be granted citizenship. Bertholf saw to it that enlisted men of the Revenue-Cutter Service were included in the act. Acting on Bertholf's recommendation that year, Congress also provided for Public Health Service physicians aboard large cruising revenue cutters. These medical officers would provide health care not only for crew members of the cutters but also for the crews of American vessels engaged in deep-sea fisheries. Bertholf directed that the revenue cutter *Androscoggin* be the first vessel to be fitted with a large sick bay and the necessary medical outfit to provide such care.[35]

Meanwhile, the bill to create the Coast Guard continued to wend its way through Congress. On 26 May 1913 it was referred to the Senate's Committee on Commerce for study. The committee would not report it out to the Senate until 27 February 1914. Two weeks later, the Senate passed "An Act to Create the Coast Guard" on 12 March. The bill was then sent to the House, where it was referred to the Interstate and Foreign Commerce Committee.

Bertholf was called to testify before the latter committee during its deliberations in May. Members of the committee questioned him about making the Life-Saving Service a part of a military organization and asked what would happen to the Life-Saving Service's superintendent if it were merged with the Revenue-Cutter Service to form the Coast Guard. Bertholf reassured the congressmen that the merger would benefit the members of the Life-Saving Service. He also emphasized the lifesaving duties of the Revenue-Cutter Service: the service rescued mariners in distress from cutters at sea while the Life-Saving Service rescued mariners in distress from stations ashore.[36] Shortly after his appearance before the committee, its members went on summer recess. By fall, World War I had begun in Europe.

In addition to witnessing the beginning of a worldwide conflict, 1914 was an election year. Members of the House of Representatives had other things on their minds and might have ignored the bill had not President Wilson personally intervened. At Secretary McAdoo's request, Wilson wrote in December 1914 to the House Democratic leader:

Dear Mr. Underwood:

> *I hope that you will not think I am unduly burdening you if I write to express my very great interest in the bill which has been passed by Senate and is pending in the House which provides for the consolidation of the Revenue-Cutter and Life-Saving Services. It is of the highest consequence for the efficiency of both services that this bill should pass, and I hope that some chink may be found for it even in the rush hours of the House Calendar.*[37]

President Wilson addressed a similar letter to Representative William C. Adamson, the chairman of the House Interstate Commerce Commission.[38]

The House finally took up the bill on 20 January and after a brief debate passed it by a vote of 212 to 79, with some minor amendments, and sent it back to the Senate. The Senate concurred on 22 January. On 28 January 1915 the Senate and House of Representatives enacted into law "An Act to Create the Coast Guard" (Public Law 239). Under its provisions the existing Revenue-Cutter Service and Life-Saving Service were combined to create the U.S. Coast Guard, "which shall constitute a part of the military forces of the United States and which shall operate under the Treasury Department in time of peace and operate as a part of the Navy, subject to the orders of the Secretary of the Navy, in time of war or when the President shall so direct." Bertholf more than likely took pleasure in the fact that after 125 years during which the service had performed so many military duties, it would finally be called "a military service."

Bertholf had played a key role in the battle to save the Revenue-Cutter Service and merge it with the Life-Saving Service, but his term of appointment was almost over. He was not sure whether his military career would end with the merger or whether he would be appointed as the commandant of the new U.S. Coast Guard and be allowed to play a crucial role in the new service's formation. His uncertainty did not last for long.

~9~

COMMANDANT, U.S.
COAST GUARD

*A*t the same time the Coast Guard was being created by the merger of the Revenue-Cutter Service and Life-Saving Service, Bertholf's four-year term as commandant of the Revenue-Cutter Service was ending. Unlike the case with his initial appointment, Bertholf did not discuss the matter of his reappointment with the secretary of the treasury, nor did he directly or indirectly ask anyone within or outside the service to boost his candidacy. As his term came to an end, Assistant Secretary Byron R. Newton, who directly oversaw the Revenue-Cutter Service/Coast Guard, sent for Bertholf to discuss the possibility of his reappointment. Bertholf advised Newton that he was not asking for reappointment but would not decline it if it were offered. If his service as commandant had been satisfactory, the secretary would naturally be inclined to reappoint him. If his performance had not been satisfactory, there was no reason why he should be reappointed.[1]

Assistant Secretary Newton wrote Secretary William McAdoo on 6 February that while several of the officers eligible for the post would probably do well as commandant, "there is not one of them so well equipped to carry forward the work of whipping the Coast Guard into shape as the present incumbent. I know from my intimate touch with both branches of the consolidated service, that he has the full confidence and respect of the officers and men."[2] McAdoo and President Wilson concurred. Bertholf was no doubt gratified that his name was submitted to Congress for appointment as the captain-commandant of the Coast Guard. On 19 June 1915 he was reappointed.

Bertholf's reappointment was greeted with approval in the press, which portrayed him as a man's man.

> There is nothing of the quarter-deck dandy about Capt. E. P. Bertholf. His years in the service which have been consumed in all sorts of dangerous enterprise, from driving a cutter in the teeth of a roaring Nor'wester . . . to the pursuit of the now vanished but once dangerous seacian, the Raiders of the Seal Rookeries, have left him pretty much "all man."[3]

Speaking of Bertholf's leadership style the article stated,

> Physically he is as well equipped as any Bucko-Mate who ever depended upon the brawn and strength of his hard-hitting fists to hold a crew of "scattermouche" bullies to heel.
>
> His mouth and eyes, too, are those of a man who commands, while his voice holds that strong timbre which can carry a hail, above the shriek of wind and crash of water, clear to the fore-top-gallant yard.

In an era that valued masculinity, Bertholf had achieved the ultimate goal of being recognized as "pretty much 'all man.'"[4]

One of Bertholf's first challenges as commandant of the Coast Guard was to overcome the doubts of those who questioned the wisdom of merging a military service with a civilian one and those who feared that the proud traditions of the two services would be lost in the merger. Those who feared that the old Life-Saving Service would lose its identity when it became part of the Coast Guard should have been reassured by the form of the organization that Bertholf established. Bertholf decided to amalgamate the personnel of the two services gradually, and initially the two services were joined only at the top. District superintendents, keepers, and surfmen would have been out of their element aboard a cutter, and lifesaving station complements were too small to permit the inclusion of specialist petty officers from the cutter service. There was little exchange of personnel between the two former services, and probably little feeling of unity, as well. Seventy-eight-year-old Sumner Kimball, the last head of the Life-Saving Service, retired on three-quarters salary when his service merged with the Revenue-Cutter Service. Bertholf detailed the chief of the operations division at headquarters, Oliver M. Maxam, for ten years Kimball's assistant, to oversee the day-to-day operations of the lifesaving branch of the Coast Guard.

Because the Coast Guard was one of the nation's armed forces, Bertholf utilized the military system of the former Revenue-Cutter Service as the basis for its organization. He was probably gratified to observe how readily the former Life-Saving Service personnel adapted themselves to the new arrangement. Appointments as commissioned officers, warrant officers, and petty officers were issued to the district superintendents, keepers, and number-one surfmen, respectively, and the remaining surfmen were regularly enlisted in the Coast Guard.

The first headquarters of the Coast Guard in Washington, D.C., was at the former headquarters of the Revenue-Cutter Service in the Munsey Building. Bertholf organized his staff into five divisions: operations, material, construction and repair, engineering, and inspection. The clerical forces formerly employed by both services were assigned to appropriate duties among the several divisions. Bertholf ordered that the distinctive Revenue-Cutter Service ensign become the distinctive flag of Coast Guard cutters. Established in 1799 in accordance with Congress's act of 2 March 1799, the ensign consisted of "sixteen perpendicular stripes, alternate red and white, the Union of the Ensign to be the Arms of the United States in dark blue on a White Field." In 1910 an executive order directed that the emblem of the Revenue-Cutter Service, in blue and white, be placed on a line with the lower edge of the union and over the center of the seventh vertical stripe.

Some of his fellow Revenue-Cutter Service officers hated to lose the name by which their service had been known for more than 100 years. Bertholf, however, believed that the name had been for many years a misnomer. He wrote to the wife of a good friend and fellow officer:

Coast Guard is the logical name for the old Revenue Cutter Service as well as the new combination, and it is a logical and direct successor of the old "revenue cutter service," so that we may fairly claim not to have lost our history, even if the particular name which we temporarily bore has been changed. The vessels will always be known as cutters and the name "cutter" still remains to indicate the floating activities of the Coast

Guard and since it is simply a continuation of the old service in that respect, we may still fairly claim to have been born in 1790.[5]

By August 1915 Bertholf was able to report to Secretary McAdoo that the organization of the new service had "progressed satisfactorily." He had convened a board of officers from both branches to revise the regulations of the two services and combine them into new regulations for the Coast Guard. As quickly as each chapter of the regulations was completed, Bertholf promulgated it to the service at large in the form of a general order.[6]

Most of the nations of Europe were at war when President Woodrow Wilson signed the legislation creating the U.S. Coast Guard on 28 January 1915. Bertholf's attention thus quite naturally focused on the enabling act's provision that the new service would at all times be an armed force of the United States and that it would "operate as a part of the Navy, subject to the orders of the Secretary of the Navy, in time of war or when the President shall so direct." Although it seemed unambiguous at first sight, the language of this provision left unanswered several questions about the Coast Guard's place within the Navy Department. Nor could past experience provide useful guidance, for while individual revenue cutters had operated with naval forces in five of the nation's nineteenth-century wars, the Revenue-Cutter Service itself had remained under the Treasury Department's control during peace and war alike.

At the request of the secretary of the treasury, Secretary of the Navy Josephus Daniels appointed Capt. William H. G. Bullard, head of the navy's Radio Service, to confer with Bertholf and recommend measures necessary to facilitate the efficient functioning of the Coast Guard within the Department of the Navy. Bertholf and Bullard, meeting for the first time on 22 December 1915, carefully considered how the Coast Guard could best be utilized by the Navy Department in the nation's defense.

The provisions of the law that established the Coast Guard allowed the secretary of the navy to direct the activities of the Coast Guard by giving orders to individual Coast Guard officers, but it did not specify any means for active cooperation of the two forces themselves. That is, there was no provision whereby officers of the two services could serve on the same ship or on ships in the same organization. Bertholf therefore recommended, with Bullard's concurrence, that an executive order be issued as follows:

> Whenever in accordance with the Act of Congress, approved on January 28, 1915, entitled "An Act to create the Coast Guard . . . ," either on the formal declaration of war, or when the President shall so direct, the Coast Guard shall operate as part of the Navy, subject to the orders of the Secretary of the Navy, Officers of the Coast Guard and of the Navy shall take rank with each other in accordance with existing laws, and all shall be subject to existing U.S. Navy Regulations and Instructions except where these conflict with laws specifically applicable to the Coast Guard and made so applicable by the Act of January 28, 1915.[7]

Bertholf recommended very close cooperation between the two services, especially during training exercises. When Coast Guard vessels were not urgently needed for their own particular duties, Bertholf wanted them to cruise as part of a navy squadron or be included in navy fleet exercises. He wanted his men to conduct regular target practice with the guns mounted on the various Coast Guard vessels, and he wanted the training to be as similar as possible to that used by the navy. Bertholf also favored a regular exchange of junior officers between the two services. Coast Guard officers would receive training in navy gun and torpedo divisions, and navy officers would gain valuable experience in boat handling and seamanship.[8] Many in the Coast Guard agreed with Bertholf. Some advocated assigning twenty or thirty officers to the navy's Atlantic and Pacific fleets for one month of each year to increase the military value of the Coast Guard. If the Coast Guard was going to serve as part of the navy, they said, its officers ought to learn at first hand something about the navy's ship-handling methods.[9]

Although Bertholf and Bullard's recommendations were not implemented because of the rapid expansion of the navy and the serious shortage of trained personnel brought about by the war in Europe, Bertholf continued to prepare the Coast Guard for service with the navy. He compiled tactical data on cutters and completed mobilization plans in March 1917.[10] Some Coast Guard units did take part in navy preparedness exercises, and harbor cutters helped to ensure security when new warships were launched in the major Atlantic coast ports.

On 20 September 1916 President Wilson appointed Bertholf chairman of the newly formed Inter-departmental Board of International Service of Ice Observation, Ice Patrol, and Ocean Derelict Destruction. At its first meeting, on 14 October 1916, the board resolved to recommend that Congress increase the Coast Guard's appropriation by eight thousand dollars for 1917 and by ten thousand dollars for 1918 "for the purpose of carrying on the work of ice observation during that fiscal year." The additional funding would allow the Coast Guard to purchase scientific instruments and hire scientifically trained observers to accompany the cutters detailed for ice patrol and ice observation duty.[11]

In February 1917 Imperial Germany resumed unrestricted submarine warfare against all merchant ships in British waters and those en route to the British Isles. On 6 April 1917 President Wilson asked Congress to declare that a state of war existed between the United States and Imperial Germany. Later that same day the naval wireless station at Arlington flashed a three-word dispatch to all Coast Guard units: "Plan One Acknowledge." Held in confidence at all Coast Guard units at this time, Plan One transferred the entire Coast Guard to the Department of the Navy. On receipt of the order, most Coast Guard activities and cutters came under the control of the naval districts in which they were located.

Individual revenue cutters had cooperated with the navy and distinguished themselves in all of the nation's previous wars, most recently in the Spanish-American War, but now, the entire Coast Guard would "operate as a part of the Navy, subject to the orders of the Secretary of the Navy." Although Bertholf, in his earlier meetings with Captain Bullard, had tried to foresee and resolve the problems the temporary merger was likely to entail, for the most part the newly formed Coast Guard would be steaming into uncharted waters as potentially hazardous for the young service as the Bering Sea and Arctic Ocean had been for the *Bear*. Bertholf would be at the helm during this critical time, and his decisions, not always popular, would shape the future relationship between the Coast Guard and the navy.

Fortunately, the orders directing the Coast Guard to operate as a part of the navy contained some specific guidance for Bertholf, who was "directed to continue until further orders the interior administration of the Coast Guard in all respects the same as when operating under the Treasury Department. All Coast Guard administration officers and office forces will be retained in present quarters and will perform their present functions."[12] In nearly all matters in which the Coast Guard was involved, Bertholf acted in an advisory capacity to the Navy Department.

All incoming correspondence affecting Coast Guard forces was referred to Bertholf for his recommendations. Outgoing correspondence affecting the Coast Guard was also sent to Bertholf for appropriate action or review. Commandant Bertholf at Coast Guard Headquarters also retained responsibility for the training academy in New London, Connecticut; the depot at Curtis Bay, Maryland; the supervisor of lifeboats; and for all Coast Guard stores. Cutters assigned to the Bering Sea Patrol and to cadet practice cruises also remained under his control. All other operations and cutters came under the operational control of the navy.

At the time of the transfer, the Coast Guard had fifteen cruising cutters, 223 commissioned officers, and 4,500 men. These now augmented the navy, which at the time had 197 ships in commission and 65,777 officers and men. Bertholf, the highest-ranking officer in the Coast Guard at the time, was the only Coast Guard officer to hold the rank equivalent to a navy captain.

The most immediate problem Bertholf faced involved personnel. The Revenue-Cutter Service had relied extensively on foreign-born seaman, but many of these men had departed, by discharge or desertion, for their homelands when the war began in Europe. Local recruitment by Coast Guard commanding officers provided a minimum of enlisted men, but when cutter complements were increased to wartime levels early in 1917, the service was forced to open recruiting offices. In the end, only conscription, beginning in June 1917, brought in enough men to meet the Coast Guard's needs. Recruits were sent to the academy at New London for outfitting and training before being assigned to ships or stations.

The war accelerated the training course at the academy. The course of instruction for line cadets was reduced from three to two years, and that for cadet engineers to about nine months. In addition to the regular work of training young men to become officers, a system of intensive training for ordinary seamen, buglers, and radio operators was established at the academy.[13] The dozen or so cadets on hand at the academy when war was declared were put to work helping to train the flood of Coast Guard seaman recruits. The *Itasca*, which had served as the academy's training vessel since 1907, was sent off to regular wartime patrol and the decrepit *Onondaga* took its place as the academy's training ship.[14]

Bertholf also faced the challenge of retaining the Coast Guard's recruits. At the completion of their one-year enlistments, many took their discharges in order to enlist in another branch of the armed forces where they thought chances for promotion were better. In the summer of 1918 enlistments were extended for the duration of the war, but not to exceed three years.[15]

Captain-Commandant Bertholf's hope that the ships' companies of Coast Guard cutters could be kept intact during the war was dashed when Naval Reserve Force officers were assigned to cutters for training. The navy's Bureau of Navigation asked that Coast Guard officers be made available for service in yachts being converted to antisubmarine vessels. Within a few months the practice became general, and Coast Guard officers found themselves serving in a variety of small combatants, transports, and auxiliary ships, their places on the cutters taken by naval reservists. The Bureau of Navigation was increasingly in need of officers for sea duty, and Bertholf feared that Coast Guard cutters in home waters would become mere training ships for the Naval Reserve Force, with only their Coast Guard commanding officers, executive officers, and engineers permanently assigned to them.[16]

Less than a month after the United States declared war on Germany, six U.S. destroyers crossed the Atlantic, entered the Celtic Sea gateway to wartime Britain and the battlefields of France, and arrived at Queensland (today Cobh) in southern Ireland. They were the first of many American ships to join the British in protecting Allied shipping from submarine attacks.[17] Since 1 February 1917, when Berlin resumed unrestricted undersea warfare, German submarines had swarmed the seas. Losses of Allied and neutral merchant ships were growing, and the Allies were feeling the pinch of lost supplies by the time the United States joined the war. The British were holding the bulk of their naval forces, including destroyers, facing the North Sea to meet any further sortie of the German High Seas Fleet (only beaten back, not decisively defeated, at Jutland the year before). American naval vessels were needed desperately for convoy escort.[18]

On 30 July 1917, six of the Coast Guard's larger cutters—the *Algonquin*, *Manning*, *Ossipee*, *Seneca*, *Tampa*, and *Yamacraw*—were ordered to be fitted out for "distant service" in an unspecified region. These six "cruising cutters" ranged in length from the 165-foot *Ossipee* to the 205-foot *Algonquin* and *Manning*. The *Algonquin*, commissioned in 1889, was the oldest, and the *Ossipee* was the newest, having been commissioned in 1914. All were single-screw steel vessels.[19] Most of these cutters had already received wartime batteries of 3-inch guns; now they were provided with depth charges as well. In August and September, all six cutters were sent to Gibraltar for service as ocean escorts with slow convoys sailing between the United Kingdom and the Mediterranean. The *Ossipee* arrived on 30 August 1917, followed by the *Seneca* on 4 September 1917. The *Manning* and *Yamacraw* arrived later that month. The *Algonquin* and the *Tampa,* both delayed by duties assigned en route, arrived in October. They would become Squadron 2 of Division 6 of the Atlantic Fleet Patrol Forces under the command of Rear Adm. Henry B. Wilson. Admiral Wilson commanded this force until November, when he was succeeded by Rear Adm. Albert P. Niblack, who retained the command through the remainder of the war.[20]

Back at home, Bertholf was fighting for better working conditions for his administrative force at Coast Guard Headquarters. The Treasury Department had leased the entire fourth floor of the Munsey Building and assigned it to Bertholf and his staff, but some of the rooms were too cold to work in during the winter. On several occasions it had been necessary for the clerks to move out of one room because of the low temperature. Bertholf argued that this situation was detrimental to the health of his staff and seriously interfered with the work of the office.[21] He requested that thirteen thousand square feet of floor space in the proposed Treasury Annex at the corner of Pennsylvania Avenue and Madison Place be assigned to the Coast Guard. The Treasury Department replied that space would probably not be available in the new building and instead leased two floors in the Bond Building as a temporary home for Bertholf and his staff.[22]

Although the navy would later argue to the contrary, Bertholf remained adamant throughout the war that while Coast Guard vessels were under the operational control of the navy, those vessels had not been "taken over" by the navy. All Coast Guard units were still officered and manned by Coast Guard personnel with one exception: junior officers of the Naval Reserve Force had been assigned to Coast Guard units to fill vacancies left when Coast Guard officers were assigned to naval units. In a few cases enlisted men of the Naval Reserve Forces had been temporarily assigned to Coast Guard units until they could be replaced by men drafted to serve in the Coast Guard.[23]

The performance of Coast Guard units and personnel during the war brought much glory and pride to its commandant. The six Coast Guard cutters serving in European waters performed valiantly in protecting the ships in their convoys from enemy submarines. The Coast Guard suffered its greatest casualty of the war when the *Tampa* was lost with all hands in European waters on 26 September 1918; 115 men, of whom 111 were Coast Guard personnel, were killed when the *Tampa* went down. An additional 81 Coast Guardsmen lost their lives in the war due to accident or illness. Because only 8,835 men served in the Coast Guard during the war, the service suffered a higher percentage of casualties than any other branch of the armed forces.[24]

Coast Guardsmen stationed on the East Coast of the United States kept a constant watch for German U-boats. Recognizing that lifesaving station and lighthouse personnel could serve effectively as coast watchers while performing their regular duties, the navy urged the expansion of the communication system to include all such installations on the nation's seacoasts, to be operated in conjunction with naval radio stations. Such an undertaking required full-time supervision, so Bertholf ordered 1st Lt. Russell R. Waesche (who would become the commandant of the Coast Guard during World War II) to Washington to head the newly established communication division at Coast Guard Headquarters. Under Waesche's direction, additional lines were laid and strung, and by mid-1919 the system had 416 miles of submarine cable and 3,255 miles of overhead wire providing telephone service to 282 Coast Guard stations, 44 Coast Guard units and offices, 139 lighthouses and lightships, 22 naval radio compass stations, and 56 other governmental offices.[25]

Coast Guardsmen were also involved in countering German sabotage within the United States, the most dramatic example of which occurred on 30 July 1916 at Black Tom Island, New Jersey, a major shipping point for explosives for the war in Europe. The explosion destroyed thirteen large brick warehouses, eighty-five loaded freight cars, six piers, and one hundred barges. Sabotage was the suspected cause.[26] The explosion in New York harbor demonstrated how vulnerable American ports were to sabotage. The Espionage Act, adopted in June 1917, transferred the responsibility for ship movements and anchorages within harbors from the U.S. Army Corps of Engineers to the secretary of the treasury. Even though the Coast Guard was now in the Department of the Navy, the treasury secretary appointed senior Coast Guard officers as "captains of the port" to carry out these duties at New York, Philadelphia, Norfolk, and Sault Sainte Marie. On 8 April 1918 Captain-Commandant Bertholf was appointed the chairman of the Board on Anchorage and Movements of Vessels, an organization charged with establishing rules and regulations to ensure the safety and security of vessels in U.S. harbors, especially those loading or unloading munitions. Those regulations would be enforced by the captains of the port under Bertholf's supervision.

Under a system developed by Capt. Godfrey L. Carden, the captain of the port of New York, harbor craft placed detachments of Coast Guardsmen onboard vessels arriving to load explosive cargoes, and the men remained onboard to assure adherence to the regulations and to prevent unauthorized persons from boarding. Ship movements between the munitions piers on the New Jersey shore and the principal explosives anchorages in Gravesend Bay at the western end of Long Island were scheduled carefully to eliminate the danger of collision.

An enormous amount of high explosives bound for the battlefields of Europe passed through the port of New York. The Coast Guard guarded against sabotage and supervised the safe loading of all those munitions, and those at Philadelphia and Norfolk as well. There were no incidents like the explosion that rocked Halifax, Nova Scotia, on 6 December 1917, when the Norwegian steamer *Imo* collided with the French *Mont Blanc* in the harbor. The French steamer, carrying five thousand tons of high explosives, caught fire and exploded, killing an estimated 1,635 people in the harbor vicinity, injuring 9,000, and damaging or destroying property valued at thirty-five million dollars. Some 350,000 tons of shells, dynamite, high explosives, and ammunition were loaded on 1,698 vessels in New York harbor during the war without the loss of a single life or so much as a minor mishap or explosion because of the careful supervision and ceaseless vigilance of Coast Guardsmen. The total value of these dangerous cargoes was estimated at a half billion dollars.[27]

These Coast Guard port security activities, though not glamorous or well known, were crucial to the war effort. Commodore Bertholf visited Coast Guard port security personnel in New York in December 1918 and shared with them his philosophy on the role of the service.

As for the meaning of the Coast Guard. The fundamental reason for its existence in peace times is the conservation of life and property. In war times, your duty was the safeguarding of the loading of explosives in New York Harbor. That constant daily grind was done well, and it could only be done to your attention to duty every day. Your intelligence knew what had to be done and when it must be done, but only the discipline of this organization enabled you to do it.

Your work has been vitally necessary in order that the men over seas might have something with which to fight.

Someone asked me the other day "What is the business of the Coast Guard man?" I said, "To do his duty." To the question, "What is his duty?" I made reply, "To do that which is given him to do well." And you men have done your duty, and have done it nobly.[28]

The first steps leading to the establishment of the Coast Guard's aviation branch were taken during the war as well. Two of the earliest advocates of using aircraft for search and rescue efforts were Coast Guard lieutenants Elmer F. Stone and Norman B. Hall. They were so persuasive that by the summer of 1916 they were flying missions in a plane borrowed from its builder, the Glenn Curtiss organization. Their success led Bertholf to send Stone and five other officers to the navy's aviation school at Pensacola, Florida. In that same year, Congress authorized the Coast Guard to establish ten airbases along the U.S. seacoasts and the Great Lakes. Unfortunately, money did not accompany the authority. During the war, six commissioned Coast Guard officers qualified as naval aviators.[29] Coast Guardsmen were in charge of several navy airbases. Capt. Philip B. Eaton commanded the Chatham Naval Air Station in Massachusetts; Capt. S. V. Parker commanded the naval air station at Rockaway, Long Island; and Capt. C. E. Sugden commanded the naval air station at Ille Tudey, France, and was awarded the Chevalier of the Legion of Honor by the French government for his wartime service.[30]

The Coast Guard continued to fulfill many of its peacetime functions during the war as well. Captain-Commandant Bertholf's annual report for 1918 stated that "while work in connection with the prosecution of the war has been the paramount duty of the Coast Guard during the year, certain functions, notably those in connection with the saving of life and property, have been carried on whenever the facilities of the service have been available for the purpose." He went on to note that during the past fiscal year 1,250 persons had been saved from death by drowning, and the assistance of Coast Guard units had resulted in the saving of lives, property, or a combination of the two in 1,303 instances.[31] After pointing out that there were only three days during the entire year when a Coast Guard unit was not called on to give aid of some kind to persons in distress or property in danger, Bertholf concluded: "The versatility and adaptability of the Coast Guard personnel have been demonstrated by a marked degree by the combination of military and humanitarian duties it has been called upon to perform throughout the year."[32]

The International Ice Patrol was terminated during the war, as was the time-honored practice of winter patrolling off the Atlantic coast. The Navy Department, which now had operational control of all cutters, decided that the needs of the war took precedence over these duties and recommended that the president discontinue the patrols for the duration of the war. However, cutters patrolling or otherwise employed and naval vessels passing along the coast were available to respond to distress calls. On the West Coast, the first-class cutter *Unalga* spent the spring and summer months of 1917 and 1918 on patrol in the Bering Sea, and the old *Bear* made its usual Arctic cruises, to Point Barrow in 1917 and as far as Wainwright in 1918, when ice conditions made it impossible to reach Point Barrow. Both cutters were used for training naval reservists during the autumn and winter months.[33]

The mixing of Coast Guard and navy officers during the war created major agitation within the officer corps of the Coast Guard. When the war began, the laws in force fixing the relative ranks of the various Coast Guard officers gave the captain-commandant the relative rank of captain in the navy, ranking *with* captains. Similarly, senior captains in the Coast Guard ranked *with* commanders in the navy. The major resentment was among Coast Guard captains, who ranked next *after* lieutenant commanders in the navy. Every lieutenant commander in the navy thus outranked every Coast Guard captain. Coast Guard captains resented the fact that a naval officer who was a mere lieutenant the day before, with relatively short service afloat, would outrank the oldest and most senior Coast Guard captain on the day he was promoted to lieutenant commander. Coast Guard captains, in effect, ranked between the grades of lieutenant and lieutenant commander in the navy.[34]

Many Coast Guard officers believed that no matter how hard seagoing Coast Guard officers worked to prove their efficiency and intelligence, this question of rank was bound to generate undeserved feelings of inferiority. These officers urged Bertholf to try to change the relative rank of Coast Guard captains with regard to U.S. Navy officers. Bertholf recognized the validity of this concern and promised to try to have the law changed.[35] In September 1917, while the Coast Guard was still operating as a part of the navy, the relative rank problem was corrected. All Coast Guard officers now ranked *with* their corresponding grades in the navy. Precedence between the two services would be determined by the date of commissions in those grades.[36]

A further irritant to Coast Guard officers was the issue of temporary promotion. Congressional legislation of 22 May 1917 provided for the temporary promotion of naval officers only. As a result, Coast Guard officers of extensive service and experience found themselves junior to much younger men with whom they were serving. The Coast Guard had thirty-one captains with twenty to thirty years of seagoing experience who ranked with temporarily promoted lieutenant commanders in the navy with only a few years experience! Frequently, Coast Guard officers could not be placed in command of squadrons because of the presence of higher-ranking Naval Reserve Force officers. To make matters worse, naval officers received 10 percent additional pay for sea duty, and Coast Guard officers did not. Bertholf spoke to the chairmen of the naval committees of both the Senate and House and to the secretary of the navy about the situation. The secretary of the navy refused to advocate any legislation to provide for temporary promotions for Coast Guard officers until he became convinced that the war had made it necessary. To the dismay of his fellow Coast Guard officers, Bertholf dropped the matter there on the ground that it was not essential to the war effort and would not apply to enlisted men anyway. He was convinced that in time the law would be changed.[37]

Bertholf's position on temporary promotions was an unpopular one. He was criticized for failing to promote the interests of the service, and he lost much of the popularity he had built up while serving as commandant of the Revenue-Cutter Service. Bertholf thought any man who systematically disregarded the opinions of others was a fool, but there were limits to what he would do in order to be popular, as he explained in a letter to a close friend.

> In the matter of popularity I must say I do not hanker for it. It is a pleasure to me, as to most people, to feel that I am well liked by those over whom I am placed in authority, but I never did and I never intend to make all sorts of concessions to that end. There are two things that I strive for and have been doing so for years—I desire to be honest and fair. It is true I cannot always succeed because no one is perfect, but at

least I can try, and I know full well that, although a man shows by his acts that he is both honest and fair, will finally get his due; nevertheless, he will be misunderstood many times and severely criticized many other times, because in attempting to be honest and fair, in a general sense, he is certain to be obliged to tread on somebody's toes in a personal sense. If, in order to be popular I have to do what other people want me to do, regardless of my own convictions, then I have no desire to be popular, and I am quite sure I will never be. It is also quite natural for a man to wish others to appreciate what he has done for them, if, indeed, he has done anything. But in this connection I may say I do not expect people to appreciate what is done for them. My experience teaches me the contrary is true.[38]

Early in 1918 the Committee on Naval Affairs of the House of Representatives held hearings on H.R. 9747, "a bill to provide temporary rank for officers of the United States Coast Guard while operating as a part of the Navy during the period of the present war, and for other purposes." Among those called to testify were Rear Adm. Leigh C. Palmer, chief of the Bureau of Navigation, and Capt. William O. Watts, the judge advocate general of the Navy. Bertholf and Capt. Charles McAllister, the engineer in chief of the Coast Guard, also testified.

The navy representatives recommended temporary promotions only for Coast Guard officers who went to sea. Bertholf argued that such a proposal was unfair. He had originally suggested that every Coast Guard officer be temporarily promoted one rank, a policy rejected by naval officers, who pointed out that in the navy all promotions above lieutenant commander were based not on seniority but on a selection process. There was another problem with such mass promotions. If all Coast Guard captains were temporarily promoted to the rank of navy captain, they would be equal in rank to the captain-commandant.

Many in Congress believed that Bertholf, as the commandant of the wartime Coast Guard, should be temporarily promoted to the rank of commodore (rear admiral, lower half). Bertholf, who believed that a commandant should outrank his subordinates, agreed. Because several of his division chiefs at Coast Guard Headquarters would have rank corresponding to a captain in the navy under the proposed promotions, Bertholf argued that the commandant should have a rank not below that corresponding to commodore in the navy. He also offered the assembled congressmen his philosophy regarding the military promotion system and ambition.

> Efficient administration in a military service requires a proper distribution of officers in the several grades, and this principle is as necessary in one service as in another. The higher grades are filled by promotion from the lower grades, not for the sole purpose of gratifying ambition, but that ambition may have its legitimate opportunity. Given the opportunity for promotion and the principle of selection in making promotion, ambition acts as a spur to call forth the best in an officer. Ambition is, therefore, not an idle thing to be disregarded, but rather to be encouraged within proper limits.[39]

The secretary of the navy did not agree that Bertholf should be promoted.

> As for the promotion of the captain commandant of the Coast Guard to the rank of commodore, the department does not approve this because the captain commandant has less responsibility and less authority than before the war began. The Navy has taken over entirely the operations of the Coast Guard vessels and Coast Guard personnel, and it believes that it is injurious to the morale of the service to give increased rank except where there is increased responsibility, and then only when it is necessary to facilitate naval administration and command.[40]

Bertholf argued that the administrative duties of the commandant of the Coast Guard had increased since the war, not decreased, as shown by the growth of the clerical force at Coast Guard Headquarters from 54 to 105 persons. While it was true that navy officers directed the operations of Coast Guard units attached to navy squadrons, all accounts and orders involving Coast Guard ships and their personnel were administered and issued by Coast Guard Headquarters. When questioned as to whether he actually commanded any of the various units, Bertholf responded by noting that the ships were not under his immediate direction any more than naval ships were under the immediate direction of a bureau chief in the navy. He argued that he, like a bureau chief, had the responsibility to keep the vessels manned and in condition to operate.

Congress agreed with Bertholf and criticized the navy, saying that it sought "to practically ostracize [Bertholf] and leave him at his desk without increased responsibility." Congressmen also turned the secretary's argument against him by arguing that the peacetime Coast Guard had six thousand enlisted men and 229 officers, and thus, using the navy's criteria, was entitled to two and one-half admirals. The legislation they proposed would give the captain-commandant the rank of commodore, a rank below rear admiral.

The act of 1 July 1918 (40 Stat. Ll, 704,731) that provided for temporary promotions in the Coast Guard also authorized the president of the United States, "during the period of the present war, to promote temporarily, with the advice and consent of the United States Senate, the captain commandant of the Coast Guard to the rank of commodore in the Navy and brigadier general in the Army."[41] On 10 October 1918 the U.S. Senate confirmed the promotion for "Ellsworth P. Bertholf, captain commandant of the Coast Guard, to have the rank of Commodore in the Navy and Brigadier General in the Army, for temporary service."

On 29 October 1918 Bertholf took the oath of office and gained the rank of commodore as of 1 July 1918. He thus became the first Coast Guard flag officer (i.e., above the rank of captain). In accordance with the law, he would revert to his permanent rank of captain shortly after the war ended. Bertholf retired before the war was officially over, and therefore retired with the temporary rank of commodore and permanent rank of captain-commandant.

The Appropriations Act of 1 July 1918, under which Bertholf was promoted to commodore, also provided both sea pay and temporary promotions for Coast Guard officers, the former to be retroactive. Their difficulty in achieving status equal to that of navy officers persuaded many Coast Guard officers that their prospects would be better if their service became a permanent part of the Navy Department. That attitude would soon cause problems for Bertholf.

The congressional act that increased the pay of navy men also provided that warrant officers and enlisted men of the Coast Guard should have pay equal to the corresponding grades of the navy. The problem was that no one was sure just what those corresponding grades were. There was no direct correspondence between grades in the two services. In the old Revenue-Cutter Service, new ratings had been established as the service developed and the need for the new rating was apparent. For example, the rating of electrician had been established to cover those who operated the new wireless telegraphs aboard cutters. The Coast Guard had no rating of chief petty officer, and consequently all of the ranking petty officers in the Coast Guard now corresponded to first-class petty officers in the navy, even though they had practically the same duties as chief petty officers. Under H.R. 6979, which restored the commandant's right to create additional grades and ratings, the Coast Guard could establish a rating of chief petty officer. The bill also provided an increase in the pay of cadets at the Coast Guard Academy to equal the compensation for midshipmen at the Naval Academy.

When hostilities ceased with the signing of the armistice agreement on 11 November 1918, Coast Guard cutters were gradually released from their war duties to resume their normal peacetime missions. In 1919 the International Ice Patrol, which had been discontinued by direction of the president during the war, was resumed. The *Androscoggin* and the *Tallapoosa* took turns maintaining a continuous patrol from 1 April to 30 June 1919.

Even though the armistice had ended hostilities, the U.S. Senate, objecting to the League of Nations, had refused to ratify the Treaty of Versailles. Thus the United States was still technically at war, and the Coast Guard was still officially a part of the Navy Department. Many congressmen and members of the Wilson administration—including a young assistant secretary of the navy named Franklin D. Roosevelt—thought it should stay there.[42]

Various schemes were suggested to bring about that object, ranging from transferring the Coast Guard as a separate corps to complete amalgamation. A bill was introduced in the Sixty-fifth Congress by Congressman Guy E. Campbell of Pennsylvania to transfer the Coast Guard bodily to the Navy Department, "with the exception of such duties as pertained to customs and such harbor vessels as were engaged in connection therewith." On 13 January 1919 the House Committee on Interstate and Foreign Commerce held hearings on Campbell's bill, H.R. 13392, and also on Congressman Parker's H.J. Res. 382, which directed the Coast Guard to resume its operations under the Treasury Department.

In support of his bill to transfer the Coast Guard permanently to the U.S. Navy, Congressman Campbell called upon Coast Guard captain F. L. Austin, who claimed to speak for much of the Coast Guard's officer corps. During the war the officers had been detailed to "larger and more responsible duties on naval vessels and through the operations of the Navy," Austin said, and they had no desire "to go back to what we consider insignificant details under the Treasury Department." Many Coast Guard officers wanted a broader field of usefulness. Austin claimed that 70 percent of the Coast Guard officers were in favor of permanent transfer to the navy.

Adm. J. S. McKean, the acting chief of naval operations, testified in favor of Campbell's bill as well. Admiral McKean noted that Congress could save money by eliminating the duplications of academies, depots, general storehouses, and division headquarters of the two services. Secretary of the Navy Daniels sent a letter to the committee expressing his support for making the Coast Guard a permanent part of the Navy Department. Secretary Daniels also sent a letter urging the committee not to give favorable consideration to the alternative bill that would return the Coast Guard to the Treasury Department.

The committee then heard from Bertholf, who systematically rebutted every argument made in favor of transferring the Coast Guard to the navy. He first addressed Admiral McKean's claim that because the Coast Guard was a part of the navy in wartime, it should be in the navy during peacetime as well so as to better prepare for its responsibilities in war. Bertholf countered that while the prime function of the navy was to prepare for war, the prime functions of the Coast Guard were the activities of peace—duties and tasks that must be performed at all times. He argued that if the Coast Guard were transferred to the navy, the Treasury Department would be forced to establish a new marine service to fulfill the peacetime roles previously assigned to the Coast Guard. Bertholf reminded the committee of the ice patrol that the navy had discontinued after its first season. The Coast Guard had taken up that duty and continued it until it was necessarily suspended during the war. "One of the traditions of which the Coast Guard is justly proud," Bertholf noted, "is that no duties that have ever been assigned to the Coast Guard have been taken away from it, nor been discontinued by the Coast Guard so long as any necessity for the duty existed."[43]

Bertholf expressed surprise at hearing Coast Guard officers speak disparagingly of their own service before the committee and express a disinclination to return after the war to "insignificant duties." He conceded that the saving of life and property at sea was necessarily hard and often tedious, but it was still a grand and noble work and hardly "insignificant."

Bertholf also expressed concern over the effect of the proposed transfer on Coast Guard officers. He feared that because they had not been trained for naval service, they would not be selected for promotion in the navy. He also noted that the bill seemed to have forgotten the enlisted men of the Coast Guard. As originally proposed, the bill demoted and reduced the pay of a large number of enlisted men. Furthermore, Bertholf argued, the service's absorption into the navy would destroy the esprit de corps of the Coast Guard.

Following Bertholf's testimony, two more Coast Guard officers, Senior Capt. John Cantwell and Capt. F. S. Van Boskerck, spoke in favor of the transfer to the Navy Department. Captain Van Boskerck was especially passionate in his support for the bill. In the course of his testimony before the committee, he also criticized the Coast Guard's top leadership. In response to Bertholf's statement that the Coast Guard was a smaller and more democratic service than the navy Van Boskerk described the Coast Guard as "one of the tightest, neatest, little autocracies extant, and its destinies have been controlled by one man." That man, he said, was Engineer-in-Chief McAllister. He charged that McAllister had practically appointed every commandant named during the past twenty years and also said that McAllister had not been to sea except on a pleasure jaunt for twenty-five years. Van Boskerck was highly critical of Bertholf as well. The commandant, he said, opposed the transfer in order to retain his power over the service. Replying to Bertholf's claim that the transfer would destroy the esprit de corps of the Coast Guard, Von Boskerck claimed that the Coast Guard's esprit de corps was gone already and that Bertholf was "trying to whip them into line, and they refuse to be whipped." Van Boskerck ended with an impassioned plea to transfer the Coast Guard out of the Treasury Department, whose secretary paid little attention to it because his time was filled with matters of greater importance.

Van Boskerck had been thinking along these lines for some time. Even before the United States had entered the war, he had written an article espousing the merger of the two services. "The United States Coast Guard: Its Military Necessities," published in the *Naval Institute Proceedings,* complained of slow promotion and insufficient appropriations for Coast Guard vessels and concluded with an argument favoring the amalgamation of the Coast Guard with the navy for the purpose of increasing military efficiency. Van Boskerck stated that he personally favored making the Coast Guard a separate corps within the Department of the Navy like the Marine Corps.[44]

Concern over their social status was one reason why many Coast Guard officers wanted a permanent transfer to the navy. Navy officers had enjoyed a high status in America since colonial times. Revenue-Cutter Service officers had shared in that social status, but some feared that the recent merger with the Life-Saving Service had associated them with socially inferior personnel.[45] By becoming part of the naval officer corps these officers would ensure a higher social status for themselves.

Although he was deeply concerned by all that he had heard, Bertholf did not believe that Congress would transfer the Coast Guard to the Navy Department, because the fundamental reasons for the two services were diametrically opposed. The navy existed for the sole purpose of preparing for and fighting wars; the main purpose of the Coast Guard had no connection with war. Its usefulness in wartime was purely incidental. Prior to the war Bertholf had believed that the Coast Guard might be just as efficient operating as a part of the Navy Department as it was in the Treasury Department, provided it was maintained as a separate corps like the Marine Corps. During the course of the war, however, he had become convinced that his service would not exist for very long in the navy as a separate corps. The Marine Corps had no ships for the navy to covet; the Coast Guard did. Bertholf was convinced that the Coast Guard would remain a separate corps only if it were in a department other than the Navy Department.

As for those of his fellow Coast Guard officers who believed that self-interest dictated Bertholf's opposition to the transfer, it should have been obvious that the opposite was true. It would have been in Bertholf's self-interest to support the Campbell bill, whose provisions were distinctly advantageous to him from a monetary and rank standpoint. Under the Treasury Department Bertholf would have a rank equivalent to captain in the navy only while serving as commandant. If the Coast Guard came under the navy, he would have the permanent rank of captain. The fact that he opposed the transfer should have absolved him from suspicion that he was motivated by self-interest. In a letter to a friend, he expressed his true self-interest: his love for the Coast Guard.

> I have been in the Service nearly 35 years and this has been my sole profession in life. The Coast Guard has earned an enviable reputation both at home and abroad, and I, as a member of the Service am entitled to enjoy that reputation, and at my age and with my length of service I have

no desire to see that reputation and the traditions of the Service bundled up and packed on a back shelf, never to be heard of again.[46]

With the war now over, Bertholf was convinced that humanitarianism, not militarism, was on the minds of Congress and the American people. In that case, it would be far better for the Coast Guard to jump on the bandwagon of humanitarianism under the Treasury Department than to ally itself with militarism under the navy.[47]

Bertholf had been under the impression that his tenure as commandant would end in June 1919, and he was greatly surprised when he learned that his term would not end until January 1920. It turned out that Congress was not in session when he was reappointed commandant in June 1915, and he had been given a recess appointment. When Congress reassembled, his name was sent in and confirmed by the Senate, and he was finally appointed under a permanent commission in January 1916. Bertholf learned for the first time that his four-year term began to run from the date of his permanent appointment.[48]

Bertholf had been anticipating his retirement from active duty in the Coast Guard for some time, but he had taken no action while the nation was still at war. Leaders of the American Bureau of Shipping had been urging him to join the bureau for almost a year. Bertholf was an earnest advocate of a strong merchant marine, and the bureau's leaders felt that he could do much to promote one if he came onboard. After the armistice, Secretary of the Navy Josephus Daniels became convinced that Bertholf could be of service to the nation by joining the Bureau of Shipping as well. When Bertholf learned of the secretary's feelings, he submitted a letter requesting retirement on 30 June 1919. Believing that the secretary should be the one to announce his retirement, Bertholf said nothing to the press and shared his plans with only a few close friends in Washington.

The news of Bertholf's retirement leaked out from the Navy Department nevertheless, and it caused something of a stir. Although his decision to retire had nothing to do with the debate over permanently transferring the Coast Guard to the Navy Department, he believed the news had been leaked to suggest such a connection. In fact, he wrote his good friend Richard Crisp, "if I believed my retiring at this time would in any way seriously affect the interests of the Coast Guard I would not retire."[49] Bertholf was confident that the Coast Guard would be returned to the Treasury Department, however, and felt free to leave the service. As one might suspect, he found himself leaving the commandant's job with mixed emotions. "I find myself leaving this office with a great many regrets," he wrote to a close friend.

> The work here has been interesting and it will become more interesting when we return to the Treasury and the strings must be drawn together again. I know I am going to be lonely over in New York and I will very sadly miss the Service associations of years, but I will be interested in my new work and by keeping busy I expect to get soon used to it.[50]

On 12 June Secretary Daniels approved Bertholf's request for retirement, and on 21 June he publicly announced the retirement of Commodore Bertholf effective 30 June. Daniels also announced that Bertholf's successor had not yet been appointed.[51]

Bertholf and his wife made plans to move to New York City, where he would join the American Bureau of Shipping as a vice president. In a farewell letter to Bertholf dated 24 June the assistant secretary of the treasury told him, "You have done a great public service of which you may well be proud."

On 30 June 1919, at the age of fifty-three years, thirty-three years and eight months of it spent in Revenue-Cutter/Coast Guard service, Bertholf retired from the Coast Guard. Although he was still a temporary commodore, he would be retired for pay purposes at his permanent rank of captain-commandant. He and his wife moved from their home at 1643 Harvard Street in Washington to their new home in New York City, and Bertholf prepared to begin a new life.

⟿ 10 ⟿

A Very Short Retirement

*A*lthough there was no lack of candidates for Bertholf's position when he retired, Secretaries Daniels and Glass agreed to make no permanent appointment until the Coast Guard's future had been decided. For the first few months following Bertholf's retirement Senior Capt. Daniel P. Foley was designated the acting commandant. Foley, the second most senior officer in the Coast Guard and the senior officer at Coast Guard Headquarters after Bertholf's retirement, had served as the inspector at headquarters under Bertholf. The most senior officer in the Coast Guard, William E. Reynolds, was serving as the commander, Southern Division, in San Francisco.

Bertholf's retirement might have been detrimental to the Coast Guard's future as a separate organization under the Department of the Treasury had Carter Glass, the secretary of the treasury, not pressed the matter with the president. While Secretary of the Navy Josephus Daniels was away visiting Pearl Harbor to open a dry dock, Glass met with President Wilson to discuss the Coast Guard's future. As a result of that meeting, Wilson issued an executive order on 28 August 1919 stating that "it is hereby directed that the Coast Guard shall on and after this date operate under the Treasury Department." Bertholf was now free to enjoy his retirement, confident that the

Coast Guard had been saved from what he had considered a threat to its existence.

Just prior to his retirement Bertholf had written to Secretary Glass "to strongly urge and recommend" that Senior Capt. William E. Reynolds be appointed his successor.[1] Reynolds was the Coast Guard's most senior officer, and although one or two other officers seemed to have greater support in Congress, Glass accepted Bertholf's recommendation. After the Coast Guard had been returned to the Treasury Department he submitted Reynolds's name to the Senate, which confirmed his appointment in September.

Bertholf sent a letter of congratulations to Reynolds on 15 September. Reynolds responded by thanking Bertholf for his part in bringing about his selection and for his offer of assistance. Reynolds wrote that he wished that Bertholf lived closer to Washington so that he would be more available for consultation. Nevertheless, he continued, "I shall not hesitate to call upon you in matters the solution to which may be deferred until I may be able to communicate with you." Reynolds concluded by wishing Bertholf "success in your new undertaking, and if energy, ability, and sound judgment insure success, you will have a full measure of it."[2] Reynolds assumed the office of commandant of the Coast Guard on 2 October.

Immediately following his retirement Bertholf and his wife moved to New York. They made their home in the Bretton Hall Hotel, and Bertholf immediately became one of the vice presidents of the American Bureau of Shipping. Bertholf was joined in his new position by the Coast Guard's former chief engineer, C. A. McAllister, who also became a vice president in the American Bureau of Shipping.

Known formerly as the American Shipmasters' Association, the American Bureau of Shipping (ABS) took its present name in 1898. The bureau was the only organization in the United States that promoted safety at sea and upheld a standard of efficiency among the seagoing merchant marine personnel. It provided marine engineers, naval architects, and ship owners with world-recognized standards for the design and construction of all types of marine vessels. The bureau worked closely with the Steamboat Inspection Service in licensing officers on American merchant vessels. The Steamboat Inspection Service, created by Congress in 1838 with the power to license masters, mates, and engineers, as well as to appoint inspectors of boilers and vessels, proved ineffective in preventing boiler explosions in its early years, and the bureau provided a strong means of self-regulation in the areas of ship design and construction. By the time of the First World War the American Bureau of Shipping was in transition to an organization dedicated solely to the classification of ships.[3] Classification, by definition, certifies that a vessel is structurally sound and mechanically fit to provide for the safety of the lives and cargoes it may carry.

In 1916 Stevenson Taylor was elected president of the bureau and the bureau purchased the Great Lakes Register, which it continued to operate as the ABS Great Lakes Department. As a result of both its reorganization and a resurgence in shipbuilding in the United States during World War I, the ABS experienced a period of growth and intense activity. It classified the majority of American ships built to meet the demands of the war and was well on its way to becoming an irreplaceable institution on the American maritime scene.

Between 1917 and 1919, when Bertholf joined it, the American Bureau of Shipping had become an international organization, signing agreements with the British Corporation for the Survey and Registry of Shipping in 1917, with Registro Italiano Navale of Italy in 1918, and with Teikoku Kaiji, the Imperial Japanese Marine Corporation, in 1919. These agreements allowed the reciprocal use of each organization's surveyors and was the bureau's first effort to promote classification on an international level.[4]

In 1921 the American Bureau of Shipping began regular publication of the *Bulletin* to supply up-to-date information on the scope of its services. By the end of that year the percentage of American-classed tonnage rated by the bureau had grown to approximately 80 percent, up from 8.5 percent in 1916.[5]

Bertholf had an important role to play in the bureau's expansion. Shortly after he went to work for the bureau, Congress passed the Merchant Marine Act of 1920 (H.R. 10378) designating the ABS the official classification organization to be consulted by every U.S. government agency.[6] The act, passed by both houses of Congress on 5 June 1920, created a U.S. Shipping Board, repealed certain emergency shipping legislation passed during World War I, and allowed the government to sell surplus ships to private American ship companies.

Bertholf's duties with the American Bureau of Shipping left him more time for leisure activities than he had had while in uniform. Shortly after moving to New York he joined the Order of the Midnight Sun, most likely an organization for those who had served in the Arctic region.[7] The group is no longer in existence, but at the time it provided Bertholf with the opportunity to compare experiences with others in a social setting. According to an article published by W. S. Harwood in 1897, the turn of the century was "the Golden Age of Fraternity." By Harwood's count, more than three hundred different fraternal orders boasted a total membership of 5.5 million American men out of a total male population of about 19 million. The majority were probably men like Bertholf, members of the white-collar middle class.[8]

After he retired from the Coast Guard Bertholf also developed an interest in genealogy and began researching and compiling his family's history. During 1921 he completed his work and donated a typewritten copy to the New York City Public Library, where it is still held.[9]

On 11 November 1921 the attention of the nation was focused on Washington, D.C., where the body of the Unknown Soldier from the Great War was carried from the Capitol Rotunda to Arlington National Cemetery and interred with full military honors on the third anniversary of the armistice in Europe. Presidents Harding, Taft, and Wilson participated in the ceremony. In New York City on that same cool autumn day, Ellsworth Bertholf died suddenly of a heart attack (angina pectoris) at his residence in the Bretton Hall Hotel. His death was a shock to his wife and friends. He was only fifty-five years old and had been active and energetic until about ten days before his death. He was survived by his wife and married stepdaughter, Mrs. Burnard Smyth of Orange, New Jersey.[10]

The *New York Times* headlined his obituary: "Com. E. P. Bertholf, Arctic Hero, Dead: Congress Gave Him a Gold Medal for His Rescue of 265 Whalers Caught in the Ice." The obituary claimed that Bertholf "was known on every coast of the United States and Alaska, and knew the sea boundaries of the country as few other men."[11]

The following day Coast Guard Headquarters issued Special Order No. 21, notifying all Coast Guard personnel of the former commandant's death. The order described Bertholf's career as "an active and distinguished one" and stated that it was "largely through his efforts that the Coast Guard was created." The order ended by noting that "a useful career as an officer and a citizen is ended" and was accompanied by directions that the special order be read at a general muster at every Coast Guard unit.

In announcing Bertholf's death, the American Bureau of Shipping, noted:

> Commodore Bertholf served the United States in its Revenue Cutter and Coast Guard Service from early manhood, never failing a call to duty, no matter what the danger, always acting in a notably distinguished and at times heroic manner, as evidenced in the especial award to him by Congress of its Gold Medal of Honor. He finally reached the highest command in the Coast Guard and retained to the last his vital interest in the cause of that service.

The ABS notice went on to declare that Bertholf had given the bureau "the same conscientious and distinguished service he had always given to his country." Speaking for the American Bureau of Shipping, Stevenson Taylor, the president, concluded, "We emulate his brilliant example."[12]

Private funeral services were held for Bertholf at Saint Matthew's Episcopal Church, at 84th Street and Central Park West in New York City, at 3:00 on the afternoon of Sunday, 13 November. The rector, Rev. Frederick Burgess, presided.[13] The next morning Bertholf's body was placed on a Pennsylvania Railroad train that left New York City at 8:05. When the train arrived at Union Station in Washington, D.C., at 1:25 that afternoon, eight pallbearers from the Coast Guard depot and six senior officers from Coast Guard Headquarters were waiting to carry Bertholf's coffin to a motor hearse that conveyed it to Arlington National Cemetery.[14] Members of the official party wore service dress uniforms with overcoats, swords and belts, gray gloves, and mourning badges. The pallbearers, all senior officers at Coast Guard Headquarters, included Comdr. John C. Moore, chief of the Division of Construction and Repair and acting commandant; Engineer-in-Chief (Comdr.) Quincy B. Newman; Comdr. Andrew J. Henderson, chief of the Division of Inspection; Bertholf's School of Instruction classmate and good friend Lt. Comdr. Richard O. Crisp, the headquarters historian; aide to the commandant and future Coast Guard commandant (1924–32) Lt. Comdr. Frederick C. Billard; and Lt. Comdr. Hamlet, chief of the Personnel Division.[15] Commodore Reynolds, the commandant, was out of town at the time of Bertholf's death and burial.

Arrangements had been made with the Navy Department to have a military funeral escort, bugler, and Protestant chaplain ready when the motor hearse reached the cemetery. The navy also furnished the flag used to drape Bertholf's coffin.[16] The funeral procession made its way from the entrance gate on the northeast side of the cemetery to the burial site atop a hill in the southwest corner. Where just a few days before a huge crowd of more than 100,000 had gathered for the interment of the Unknown Soldier, only the official party was present as the Coast Guard's first commandant, Commo. Ellsworth P. Bertholf, was buried with full military honors at 3:00 P.M. in plot number 3923-ES, Section 3, of the Southern Division of Arlington National Cemetery.[17] Located just north of Miles Drive and near the top of one of the cemetery's hills, the site overlooked the Tomb of the Unknown as the mourners faced north.

Bertholf's monument, set in place on 30 December 1921, bears his name, the inscription "Commodore, U.S.C.G.," the dates of his birth and death, and the words "Congressional Medal of Honor, June 28, 1902." Lest this medal be confused with the well-known military decoration, at the top of the monument is a full-size bronze replica of the congressional gold medal of honor that Bertholf was awarded in 1902.

Seven years later, on 23 May 1928, a monument was placed on a hill about one hundred yards south of Bertholf's gravesite commemorating the U.S. Coast Guardsmen killed in action in World War I. It lists the names of all those lost aboard the *Seneca* and *Tampa*. That hill is now known as "Coast Guard Hill" at the cemetery.

Arlington National Cemetery is a fitting final resting place for Ellsworth Bertholf, a man whose life and career exemplified the highest traditions of service to country and humanity. His career took him to all the coasts of the United States and literally around the world. It brought him into contact with the Inuit people of Alaska, with Japanese sealers, with Russian government officials in Saint Petersburg and Siberia, and with major American political and naval leaders of his era.

As the last commandant of the Revenue-Cutter Service Bertholf prevented its dissolution in 1911 and later helped merge that quasi-military service with the civilian Life-Saving Service to form the U.S. Coast Guard in 1915. Bertholf was the Coast Guard's first commandant and first flag officer, and he was at the head of the service during World War I when the Coast Guard suffered the highest percentage of casualties of any American armed service. As the war ended and his military career was drawing to a close, Bertholf successfully fought to keep the Coast Guard separate from the U.S. Navy.

Part of the mission of the U.S. Coast Guard Academy, the source of the majority of Coast Guard officers, is to produce graduates who are "strong in the resolve to be worthy of the traditions of commissioned officers in the United States Coasts Guard in the service of their country and humanity." Ellsworth Bertholf is the embodiment of the best of that tradition, worthy to be remembered and honored.

~❧ Notes ❧~

CHAPTER 1. BOYHOOD

1. The records of the 79th U.S. Colored Infantry are contained in several volumes of *The Official Records of the Union Army in the War of Rebellion.*

2. Kendrick Scofield, "No Quarter-Deck Dandy Is the Commandant of Revenue Cutter Service," 16 January 1915.

3. Ibid.

4. Frances A. Westervelt, *History of Bergen County, New Jersey, 1630–1923,* 2:506–7.

5. Anthony Rotundo, "Boy Culture: Middle-Class Boyhood in Nineteenth-Century America," in *Meanings for Manhood: Constructions of Masculinity in Victorian America,* 15–16.

6. Ibid., 15–36.

7. Daniel Beard, *Hardly a Man Is Now Alive: The Autobiography of Dan Beard,* 73–78.

8. "Yearbook of Hackensack," *Bergen County Democrat,* 1915, 81.

9. See Clayton W. Woodward, *History of Bergen and Passaic Counties, New Jersey,* 183.

10. Ibid.

11. Ellsworth Bertholf, "Captain Bertholf on Prof. Haas," *Hackensack Republican,* 28 December 1916.

12. "The Death of Professor Haas," *Hackensack Republican,* 4 January 1906.

13. Bertholf, "Captain Bertholf on Prof. Haas."

14. Oliver Wendell Holmes, "Memorial Day" (1884), in *Speeches,* 11, as cited by George M. Fredrickson in *The Inner Civil War,* 219–20.

15. Theodore Roosevelt, *The Strenuous Life,* 3.

16. Howard P. Chudacoff, *The Age of the Bachelor,* 239.

17. Woodward, *History of Bergen and Passaic Counties,* 183.

18. *Hackensack Republican,* 7 July 1881.

19. Nathan Miller, *The U.S. Navy: A History,* 146.

20. *Hackensack Republican,* 11 May 1882.

21. *Hackensack Republican,* 8 June 1882, 1.

CHAPTER 2. THE CADET YEARS

1. *Annual Report of the Secretary of the Navy,* 1881.
2. The Act of 5 August 1881, *Congressional Record,* 47th Cong., 1st sess.
3. *Congressional Record,* 47th Cong., 1st sess., Senate, 4 August 1882, 6873–75, 5 August 1882, 6910; and House, 5 August 1882, 6975–78.
4. Merrill L. Bartlett, "Two Admirals for an Ensign," *Naval Institute Proceedings* (February 1998): 55–59.
5. Cadet and Conduct Record, 1881–1908.
6. Jack Sweetman, *U.S. Naval Academy.*
7. Ibid., 125–26.
8. Cadet and Conduct Record, 1881–1908.
9. Ibid.
10. Sweetman, *U.S. Naval Academy,* 119.
11. Ibid.
12. Ibid., 120–21.
13. Cadet and Conduct Record, 1881–1908.
14. Sweetman, *U.S. Naval Academy,* 104.
15. "The Hazing Cadets on Trial," *New York Times,* 1 September 1883, 5.
16. "Our Cadet," *Hackensack Republican,* 6 September 1883.
17. "Record of the proceedings of a Naval Court Martial held at the United States Naval Academy, on Monday and Tuesday, the third and fourth days of September, eighteen hundred and eighty-three, for the trial of Naval Cadet E. P. Bertholf, U.S. Navy."
18. Acting Secretary of the Navy to Ellsworth P. Bertholf, 12 September 1883, Letters and Papers of Ellsworth P. Bertholf, U.S. Coast Guard Academy Library, New London, Conn. [hereinafter Bertholf Papers].
19. "The Accused Naval Cadets," *New York Times,* 15 September 1883.
20. "'Our' Cadet Dismissed," *Hackensack Republican,* 13 September 1883.
21. Secretary of the Navy to H. K. and F. B. Thurber & Co., New York City, 3 December 1883, Bertholf Papers.
22. *Who's Who in America, 1920–21,* 11:241; E. P. Bertholf to Treasurer, Naval Academy Graduates Association, 3 June 1916, Alumni File, Records of the Naval Academy.
23. "Commodore Bertholf," *Hackensack Republican,* 17 November 1921.
24. Circular No. 29, 29 June 1885, Register of Letters Sent, 1879–1909, Records of the Coast Guard, National Archives, Washington, D.C. [hereinafter Letters Sent, USCG Records].
25. The Act of 23 June 1906 (34 Stat. L., 452) provided that "no person who has been dismissed or compelled to resign for hazing . . . shall be eligible for appointment as a cadet in the Revenue-Cutter Service."
26. Secretary of the Treasury to Capts. George Slice, George Moore, and Thomas Lay, 21 May 1885, Letters Sent, USCG Records.

27. Examining Board to Secretary of the Treasury, 3 September 1885, Letters Sent, USCG Records.

28. Donald L. Canney, *U.S. Coast Guard and Revenue Cutters, 1790–1935,* 45.

29. Worth G. Ross, "Our Coast-Guard," 917.

30. Paul Johnson and Bill Earle, "U.S. Coast Guard Academy: The First 100 Years," 2–26.

31. Ibid., 5.

32. Deck Log, USRC *Chase,* 12 April 1885.

33. *Record of Movements: Vessels of the United States Coast Guard, 1790–December 31, 1933,* 183.

34. Riley Hughes, *Our Coast Guard Academy,* 55.

35. Assistant Secretary of the Treasury to Capt. D. B. Hodgsdon, 14 May 1887, Letters Received, USCG Records.

36. *Record of Movements,* 183.

37. Capt. D. B. Hodgsdon to Assistant Secretary of the Treasury, 7 September 1887, Letters Sent, USCG Records.

38. Board of Examiners to Secretary of the Treasury, 30 November 1887, Letters Sent, USCG Records.

39. Ibid.

40. Ibid.

41. Deck Log, USRC *Levi Woodbury.*

42. Board of Examiners to Secretary of the Treasury, 30 May 1889, Letters Sent, USCG Records.

43. Deck Log, USRC *Levi Woodbury.*

CHAPTER 3. EARLY CAREER

1. Johnson and Earle, "U.S. Coast Guard Academy: The First 100 Years," 8.

2. William J. Wheeler, "Reminiscences of 'The Old Guard.'"

CHAPTER 4. THE OVERLAND RELIEF EXPEDITION

1. Dennis L. Noble and Truman R. Strobridge, "Early Cuttermen in Alaskan Waters," 81.

2. Don Black, "Last Member of Cutter Crew Recalls Arctic Rescue."

3. Ellsworth Bertholf, "The Rescue of the Whalers," 4. Much of the information in this chapter comes from this article.

4. U.S. Coast Guard, *The Coast Guard at War: Alaska III,* 19.

5. Bertholf's official report was published in *Report of the Cruise of the U.S. Revenue Cutter* Bear *and the Overland Expedition for the Relief of Whalers in the Arctic Ocean: From November 27, 1897, to September 13, 1898;* see p. 23.

6. William McKinley, address to the Senate and House of Representatives, 17 January 1899, in *Messages and Papers of the Presidents* (New York: Bureau of National Literature), 13:6352.

CHAPTER 5. GOLD, REINDEER, AND BITTER COLD

1. Much of the information about Bertholf's experiences in Alaska comes from correspondence in the Alaska File (1899–1900) of the U.S. Coast Guard Records in the National Archives.
2. Much of the information about Bertholf in Russia comes from *The Eleventh Annual Report on Introduction of Domestic Reindeer into Alaska* (Washington, D.C.: Government Printing Office, 1902).
3. Department of the Treasury to E. P. Bertholf, 21 January 1902, Letters Sent, USCG Records.
4. Bertholf to Secretary of the Treasury, 11 February 1902, Alaska File, USCG Records.

CHAPTER 6. CLIMBING THE CAREER LADDER

1. Information about Bertholf's time aboard the *Manning* is contained in Deck Log, USRC *Manning*, 1902, USCG Records.
2. Bennet, "The Life-Savers: 'For Those in Peril on the Sea,'" 61.
3. *Hackensack Republican,* 9 July 1903; and *Bergen County Democrat,* 10 July 1903.
4. Secretary of the Treasury to 1st Lieutenant Bertholf, 13 August 1904, Letters Sent, USCG Records.
5. "Com. E. P. Bertholf, Arctic Hero, Dead," *New York Times,* 12 November 1921.
6. Information about Bertholf's time aboard the *Wissahickon* is contained in the Deck Log, USRC *Wissahickon,* 1906–7, USCG Records.
7. Information about Bertholf's time aboard the *Seminole* is contained in the Deck Log, USRC *Seminole,* 1907, USCG Records.

CHAPTER 7. COMMAND AT SEA

1. Much of the information in his chapter comes from the Deck Log of the USRC *Bear,* 1908–9, USCG Records.
2. Frank W. Wead, *Gales, Ice and Men,* 193.
3. "Great Review in Pacific," *New York Times,* 29 February 1908, 6.
4. "Warships Gather for Great Parade," *New York Times,* 2 May 1908, 3.
5. *New York Sun,* 7 May 1908; see also Robert A. Hart, *The Great White Fleet,* 166.

6. "Bay Policing Adds to Grand Spectacle," *San Francisco Chronicle*, 7 May 1908, 7.

7. "Evans Takes Fleet into San Francisco," *New York Times*, 7 May 1908, 4.

8. Information on the Bering Sea Patrol for this year is contained in the Alaska File, USCG Records.

9. "The Killing of Mother Seals," *New York Times*, 8 September 1909, 8; "Saving the Seal Fisheries," *New York Times*, 27 November 1909, 8; "To Protect Sea Mammals," *New York Times*, 25 November 1909, 7.

10. See "Capture Japanese Sealer," *New York Times*, 25 July 1909, 1.

11. Bertholf to Carden, 22 January 1909, Bertholf Papers.

12. These events are described in detail in Robert Douville's unpublished article "The 1911 Campaign to be Captain-Commandant" (copy in author's files).

13. Bertholf to Carden, 22 January 1909, Bertholf Papers.

14. Carden to Bertholf, 6 March 1909, Bertholf Papers.

15. Commanding Officer, USRC *Bear*, report dated 20 August 1909, Alaska File, USCG Records.

16. Bertholf letter, 13 November 1909, claiming reimbursement for expenditure of $59.04 on 3 October, Alaska File, USCG Records.

17. Commander, Bering Sea Fleet, to Bertholf, 4 November 1909, Alaska File, USCG Records.

18. See the files of the U.S. Treasury Department, Division of Appointments, for more information on the competition to succeed Captain-Commandant Ross.

19. John F. Murphy, "Cutter Captain: The Life and Times of John C. Cantwell," undated manuscript, U.S. Coast Guard Academy Library, 130, 135–36, 138, 141.

20. Clark's letter of 6 April 1911 is in Bertholf's file in the Treasury Department, Division of Appointments.

CHAPTER 8. COMMANDANT, U.S. REVENUE-CUTTER SERVICE

1. "International Convention—Fur Seals," U.S. Statutes at Large, 62d Cong., 37, pt. 2, 1542–47.

2. House Committee on Foreign Affairs, *Hearings on H.R. 1657: The Protection of Fur Seals and Sea Otter*, 3–4 January 1912 (Washington, D.C.: Government Printing Office, 1912), 4.

3. Act of 24 August 1912 [H.R. 16571], 37 Statutes at Large, 501.

4. *Annual Report of the United States Revenue-Cutter Service, 1913*, 51.

5. 46 U.S.C. 511, 519.

6. Frederick A. Cleveland, "Report of the Commission on Economy and Efficiency," *House Documents*, 62d Cong., 2d sess., 1912, 116:269–70.

7. Ibid., 269.

8. *House Documents,* 62d Cong., 2d sess., 116:381.

9. Franklin MacVeagh to President Taft, 26 February 1912, in *House Documents,* 62d Cong., 2d sess., 116:382.

10. Bertholf to MacVeagh, 17 February 17, 1912, USCG Records.

11. *Outlook,* 10 February 1912, 296–97.

12. Chamber of Commerce of Wilmington, N.C., 29 January 1912; Chamber of Commerce of Southport, N.C., 30 January 1912, in *House Documents,* 62d Cong., 2d sess., vol. 116.

13. *New York Times,* 9 April 1912, 4.

14. "A Wreck to Be Proud Of," *New York Times,* 10 April 1912, 12.

15. Irving King, *The Coast Guard Expands, 1865–1915,* 147.

16. Bertholf to Assistant Secretary Allen, 4 January 1913, Letters Sent, USCG Records.

17. MacVeagh to Bertholf, 10 January 1913, Letters Received, USCG Records.

18. Bertholf to MacVeagh, 18 January 1913, Letters Sent, USCG Records.

19. Meyer to MacVeagh, 28 February 1913, copy in *Annual Report of the Navy Department,* 1913. Also see Paolo E. Coletta, *A Survey of U.S. Naval Affairs 1865–1917,* 186–88.

20. Letter in *Annual Report of the U.S. Revenue-Cutter Service* [hereinafter *Annual Report, USRCS*], 47.

21. Bertholf to Assistant Secretary Allen, 14 March 1913, Letters Sent, USCG Records.

22. "Few Big Icebergs Seen This Year," *New York Times,* 17 August 1913; "The Ice Patrol," *Scientific American* (May 1914): 416.

23. Letter in *Annual Report, USRCS,* 1913.

24. Jusserand to Secretary of State William J. Bryan, 27 June 1914, copy in USCG Records.

25. Redfield to MacVeagh, 7 April 1913, USCG Records.

26. *Senate Documents,* 63d Cong., 2d sess. (Washington, D.C.: Government Printing Office, 1914), 80.

27. *Annual Report, USRCS,* 1914, 90.

28. Senate Committee on Foreign Relations, hearings, 63d Cong, 2d sess. (Washington, D.C.: Government Printing Office, 1914), 199.

29. Ibid., 207.

30. *Congressional Record,* 63d Cong., 1st sess., 50, pt. 1:161.

31. Ibid., pt. 2:1735.

32. Act of 15 February 1911 (36 Statutes at Large, 906).

33. *Annual Report, USRCS,* 1912, 55.

34. *Annual Report USRCS,* 1914, 93.

35. Ibid., 94–95.

36. House Committee on Interstate and Foreign Commerce, *Hearings on S. 2337,* 63d Cong., 2d sess. (Washington, D.C.: Government Printing Office, 1914).

37. *Congressional Record,* 63d Cong., 3d sess., 1914.

38. *New York Times,* 2 January 1915, 11.

CHAPTER 9. COMMANDANT, U.S. COAST GUARD

1. Bertholf to R. O. Crisp, 26 March 1919, Bertholf Papers.

2. Newton, memorandum for the secretary, 8 February 1915, Reference Collection, USCG Headquarters.

3. Kendrick Scofield, "No Quarter-Deck Dandy Is the Commandant of Revenue Cutter Service." A photocopy of a part of this news article is in the Bertholf Papers at the Coast Guard Academy. The text of the article indicates that it was written the day after Congress passed the bill to create the Coast Guard, but I do not know where it was published.

4. Ibid.

5. Bertholf to Mrs. L. H. Crisp, 12 February 1915, Bertholf Papers.

6. *Annual Report of the U.S. Coast Guard* [hereinafter *Annual Report, USCG*], 1915, 31.

7. Bertholf to McAdoo, 20 March 1915, Letters Sent, USCG Records.

8. Ibid., 13–15.

9. F. C. Billard, "The Coast Guard in War," 82–85.

10. Newton to Secretary of the Navy, 12 January 1917, Letters Sent, USCG Records.

11. Bertholf to the President, 11 November 1916, Letters Sent, USCG Records.

12. Secretary of the Navy to Bertholf, 6 April 1917, Letters Received, USCG Records.

13. *Annual Report, USCG,* 1918, 8–9.

14. Johnson and Earle, "U.S. Coast Guard Academy: The First 100 Years," 25.

15. Bertholf to Crisp, 27 September 1917; Bertholf to Chief of the Bureau of Navigation, 22 July 1918, Letters Sent, USCG Records.

16. Ibid.

17. See J. K. Taussig, "Destroyer Experience during the Great War," *Naval Institute Proceedings* (December 1922): 2015, (January 1923): 39, (February 1923): 221, (March 1923): 383; William S. Sims, *The Victory at Sea;* Worth Bagley, "Torpedoed in the Celtic Sea," 36.

18. See Winston S. Churchill, *The World Crisis 1916–1918,* pt. 1, pp. 213–34, and pt. 2, pp. 349–74. Good statistics are given in Joseph Davies, *The Prime Minister's Secretariat, 1916–1920;* see also *British Vessels Lost at Sea, 1914–1918* (London: Her Majesty's Printing Office, n.d.); and Lord Edward Gleichen, gen. ed., *Chronology of the Great War.*

19. For details on the "cruising cutters," see *Jane's Fighting Ships,* 1914–18.

20. Sims, *The Victory at Sea,* 161.

21. Bertholf to Secretary of the Treasury, 13 December 1917, Letters Sent, USCG Records.

22. Assistant Secretary of the Treasury to Bertholf, 28 December 1917, Letters Received, USCG Records.

23. Bertholf to Bureau of Navigation, 1 June 1918, Letters Sent, USCG Records.

24. Robert L. Scheina, "The Coast Guard at War," 30.

25. Ibid., 50.

26. See Jules Witcover, *Sabotage at Black Tom: Imperial Germany's Secret War in America.*

27. Karl Baarslag, *Coast Guard to the Rescue,* 395.

28. Bertholf address at muster and inspection of Coast Guard Battalion in 9th Regiment Armory, 20 December 1918, USCG Records.

29. *Annual Report, USCG,* 1918.

30. Robert L. Scheina, "A History of Coast Guard Aviation," 13.

31. *Annual Report, USCG,* 1918.

32. Ibid.

33. *Annual Report, USCG,* 1919.

34. J. G. Ballinger to Bertholf, 19 April 1916, Letters Received, USCG Records.

35. Bertholf stated his "recognition" of the validity in Bertholf to Ballinger, 25 April 1916, USCG Records.

36. Navy Department Circular No. 28762-115, Op-28, 26 September 1917.

37. Bertholf to Crisp, 6 July 1917, Bertholf Papers.

38. Ibid.

39. Committee on Naval Affairs, 65th Cong., 2d sess., 18 February 1918, 553.

40. *Congressional Record,* 65th Cong., 2d sess., 56:8015.

41. Ibid., 732.

42. Walter C. Capron, *The U.S. Coast Guard,* 63.

43. Committee on Interstate and Foreign Commerce, *Hearing on H.R. 13392 and H.R. Res. 382,* 65th Cong., 13 January 1919, 67.

44. F. S. Van Boskerck, "The United States Coast Guard: Its Military Necessities."

45. For example, G. L. Carden to Thomas M. Moore, 27 February 1915, Carden Collection, U.S. Coast Guard Academy; and Bertholf to Mrs. L. H. Crisp, 12 February 1915, Bertholf Papers.

46. Bertholf to R. O. Crisp, 18 April 1919, Bertholf Papers.

47. Ibid.

48. Bertholf to R. O. Crisp, 26 March 1919, Bertholf Papers.

49. Bertholf to R. O. Crisp, 21 June 1919, Bertholf Papers.

50. Ibid.

51. *New York Times,* 22 June 1919, 5.

Chapter 10. A Very Short Retirement

1. Bertholf to Secretary of the Treasury, 20 June 1919, copy in Billard papers, USCG Academy.

2. Reynolds to Bertholf, 30 September 1919, Letters Sent, USCG Records.

3. *The History of the American Bureau of Shipping: 1862–1994*, 6–8.

4. Ibid., 10–11.

5. Ibid., 12.

6. *Congressional Record*, 66th Cong., 59, pt. 8:8589–8609.

7. Marquis, *Who Was Who, 1897–1942*, 1:89.

8. W. S. Harwood, "Secret Societies in America," *North American Review* 164 (May 1897), cited by Michael Kimmel in *Manhood in America: A Cultural History*.

9. Bertholf, "Ancestry of Ellsworth Price Bertholf, compiled by himself."

10. "Death of Captain Commandant E. P. Bertholf, U.S. Coast Guard Retired," typed manuscript in USCG Records.

11. Ibid.

12. *U.S. Coast Guard Academy Alumni Association Bulletin* 1, no. 6 (November–December 1921).

13. "Death of Captain Commandant E. P. Bertholf."

14. H. G. Hamlet, Memorandum for the Commandant: "Funeral Arrangements, Late Captain E. P. Bertholf, U.S. Coast Guard," 12 November 1921, USCG Records [hereinafter Hamlet Memorandum].

15. J. M. Moore, "Funeral of the Late Captain E. P. Bertholf," memorandum, 12 November 1921, USCG Records.

16. Hamlet Memorandum.

17. Records of Arlington National Cemetery.

~~*Bibliography*~~

PRIMARY SOURCES

Abstract of the Course at the Naval War College, 1895. Washington, D.C.: Government Printing Office, 1895.

Annual Report of the United States Coast Guard. Washington, D.C.: Government Printing Office, 1915, 1916, 1917, 1918, 1919, 1920.

Annual Report of the United States Revenue-Cutter Service. Washington, D.C.: Government Printing Office, 1912, 1913, 1914.

Annual Report of the U.S. Life-Saving Service. Washington, D.C.: Government Printing Office, 1904, 1906.

Beard, Daniel. *Hardly a Man Is Now Alive: The Autobiography of Dan Beard.* New York: Doubleday, Doran, 1939.

Bergen County Democrat, 1881–1921.

Bertholf, E. P. "Ancestry of Ellsworth Price Bertholf, compiled by himself." Typescript, 1921. New York City Public Library.

———. "Expedition to Siberia." Appendix to *Eleventh Annual Report on Introduction of Domestic Reindeer into Alaska,* by Sheldon Jackson. Washington, D.C.: Government Printing Office, 1902.

———. Letters and Papers. U.S. Coast Guard Academy Library, New London, Conn.

———. "The Rescue of the Whalers." *Harper's New Monthly Magazine* (June 1899): 3–24.

Crisp, R. O. *A History of the United States Coast Guard in the World War.* Washington, D.C.: Government Printing Office, 1922.

Hackensack Republican, 1881–1921.

Jackson, Sheldon. *Fifteenth Annual Report on Introduction of Domestic Reindeer into Alaska.* Washington, D.C.: Government Printing Office, 1906.

Kimball, Sumner I. *Organization and Methods of the United States Life-Saving Service.* Washington, D.C.: Government Printing Office, 1912.

Record of Movements, Vessels of the United States Coast Guard, 1790–December 31, 1933. Washington, D.C.: U.S. Coast Guard Headquarters, 1989.

Records of the United States Coast Guard. Record Group 26. National Archives and Records Administration, Washington, D.C.

Records of the United States Naval Academy. Record Group 405. U.S. Naval Academy, Annapolis, Md.

Register of the Officers, Vessels, and Stations of the United States Coast Guard. Washington, D.C.: Government Printing Office, 1909, 1917, 1918, 1919.

Regulations for the Government of the Revenue-Cutter Service of the United States. Washington, D.C.: Government Printing Office, 1894.

Roosevelt, Theodore. *The Strenuous Life.* New York: Review of Reviews Company, 1910.

Wallace, Lew. *Lew Wallace: An Autobiography.* New York: Harper & Brothers, 1906.

United States Revenue-Cutter Service. *Report of the Cruise of the U.S. Revenue Cutter* Bear *and the Overland Expedition for the Relief of the Whalers in the Arctic Ocean: From November 27, 1897, to September 13, 1898.* Washington, D.C.: Government Printing Office, 1899.

SECONDARY SOURCES

"A 'Little Navy' That Does Big Work." *Outlook,* 10 February 1912, 296–97.

Anderson, Madelyn Klein. *Sea Raids and Rescues: The United States Coast Guard.* New York: David McKay, 1979.

Baarslag, Karl. *Coast Guard to the Rescue.* New York: Farrar & Rinehart, 1937.

Baedeker, Karl. *Baedeker's Russia, 1914.* London: George Allen & Unwin, 1914.

Bagley, Worth. "Torpedoed in the Celtic Sea." *Naval History* (May–June 1997): 36–40.

"The Beginning: Academy Opens Doors 50 Years Ago at Present Site." *U.S. Coast Guard Academy Alumni Association Bulletin* (September–October 1982): 9–13.

Bell, Kensil. *"Always Ready!" The Story of the United States Coast Guard.* New York: Dodd, Mead, 1943.

Bennet, Robert F. "The Life-Savers: 'For Those in Peril on the Sea.'" *Naval Institute Proceedings* 102 (March 1976): 55–63.

Billard, F. C. "The Coast Guard in War." Journal of the United States Coast Guard Association 1 (January–March 1917): 82–85.

Birkett, F. J. "The Old Bear of the North." *Marine Corps Gazette* (May 1935): 7–10.

Bixby, William. *Track of the Bear.* New York: David McKay, 1965.

Black, Don. "Last Member of Cutter Crew Recalls Arctic Rescue." *Spokane Chronicle,* 6 July 1963.

Bloomfield, Howard V. L. *The Compact History of the United States Coast Guard.* New York: Hawthorne Books, 1968.

Brown, Riley. *The Story of the Coast Guard: Men, Wind and Sea.* Garden City, N.Y.: Blue Ribbon Books, 1939.

Burroughs, Polly. *The Great Ice Ship BEAR: Eighty-nine Years in Polar Seas*. New York: Van Nostrand, 1970.

Canney, Donald L. *U.S. Coast Guard and Revenue Cutters, 1790–1935*. Annapolis: Naval Institute Press, 1995.

Capron, Walter C. *The U.S. Coast Guard*. New York: Franklin Watts, 1965.

Chudacoff, Howard P. *The Age of the Bachelor: Creating an American Subculture*. Princeton: Princeton University Press, 1999.

Churchill, Winston S. *The World Crisis 1916–1918*. London: Thornton Butterworth, 1927.

Cochran, C. S. "The 'Bear.'" *Naval Institute Proceedings* 55 (May 1929): 411–16.

Coletta, Paolo E. *A Survey of U.S. Naval Affairs 1865–1917*. Lanham, Md.: University Press of America, 1987.

Crane, John, and James F. Kieley. *United States Naval Academy: The First Hundred Years*. New York: McGraw-Hill, 1945.

David, Evan J. *Our Coast Guard: High Adventure with the Watchers of Our Shores*. New York: D. Appleton-Century, 1937.

Davies, Joseph. *The Prime Minister's Secretariat, 1916–1920*. Newport, Monmouthshire: R. H. Johns, 1951.

Eldridge, F. R. *"They Have to Go Out": An Historical Sketch of the U.S. Coast Guard, 1790–1946*. Washington, D.C.: U.S. Coast Guard, 1953.

Evans, Stephen H. *The United States Coast Guard 1790–1915: A Definitive History*. Annapolis: Naval Institute Press, 1949.

Filene, Peter. *His/Her Self: Sex Roles in Victorian America*. Baltimore: Johns Hopkins University Press, 1986.

Fredrickson, George M. *The Inner Civil War: Northern Intellectuals and the Crisis of the Union*. New York: Harper & Row, 1965.

Gleichen, Lord Edward, gen. ed. *Chronology of the Great War*. 3 vols. London: Countwhile, 1918.

Grosvenor, Gilbert H. "Reindeer in Alaska." *National Geographic Magazine* (April 1903): 126–48.

Gurney, Gene. *The United States Coast Guard: A Pictorial History*. New York: Crown, 1973.

Halpern, Paul G. *A Naval History of World War I*. Annapolis: Naval Institute Press, 1994.

Hart, Robert A. *The Great White Fleet: Its Voyage around the World, 1907–1909*. Boston: Little, Brown, 1965.

Hilkey, Judy. *Character Is Capital: Success Manuals and Manhood in Gilded Age America*. Chapel Hill: University of North Carolina Press, 1997.

The History of the American Bureau of Shipping, 1862–1994. 4th ed. New York: American Bureau of Shipping, 1995.

Hughes, Riley. *Our Coast Guard Academy: A History and Guide*. New York: Devin-Adair, 1944.

Johnson, Paul, and Bill Earle. "U.S. Coast Guard Academy: The First 100 Years." *U.S. Coast Guard Academy Alumni Association Bulletin,* Centennial Issue, 1976.

Johnson, Robert Erwin. *Guardians of the Sea: History of the United States Coast Guard, 1915 to the Present.* Annapolis: Naval Institute Press, 1987.

Kaplan, H. R., and James F. Hunt. *This Is the Coast Guard.* Cambridge, Md.: Cornell Maritime Press, 1972.

Kimmel, Michael. *Manhood in America: A Cultural History.* New York: Free Press, 1996.

King, Irving H. *The Coast Guard Expands 1865–1915: New Roles, New Frontiers.* Annapolis: Naval Institute Press, 1996.

Marvin, D. P. "New United States Coast Guard Academy." *Coast Guard Magazine* (August 1932): 4–6.

Maxam, Oliver M. "The Life-Saving Stations of the United States Coast Guard." *Naval Institute Proceedings* 55 (May 1929).

Miller, Nathan. *The U.S. Navy: A History.* Annapolis: Naval Institute Press, 1997.

Noble, Dennis L. *Alaska and Hawaii: A Brief History of U.S. Coast Guard Operations.* Washington, D.C.: U.S. Coast Guard Historian's Office, 1991.

———. *That Others Might Live: The U.S. Life-Saving Service, 1878–1915.* Annapolis: Naval Institute Press, 1974.

Noble, Dennis L., and Truman R. Strobridge. "Early Cuttermen in Alaskan Waters." *Pacific Northwest Quarterly* 48 (July 1987): 74–82.

Odom, Curtis B., "Let's Transfer the Coast Guard to the Department of ———: A History of Proposed Moves." *U.S. Coast Guard Academy Alumni Association Bulletin* (March–April 1983): 2529.

Perry, Glen. *Watchmen of the Sea.* New York: Charles Scribner's Sons, 1938.

Porter, Kent. "Triumph and Tragedy of the *Bear.*" *Sea Classics* (January 1976): 51–60.

Rachlis, Eugene. *The Story of the U.S. Coast Guard.* New York: Random House, 1961.

Reckner, James R. *Teddy Roosevelt's Great White Fleet.* Annapolis: Naval Institute Press, 1988.

Reed, Byron L. "The Contribution of the Coast Guard to the Development of Alaska." *Naval Institute Proceedings* 55 (May 1929): 406–10.

Reynold, George Richard. "The Coast Guard in the Northwest: 1854–1900." Master's thesis, University of Washington, 1968.

Ross, Worth G. "Our Coast-Guard." *Harper's New Monthly Magazine* 81 (November 1886): 917.

Rotundo, Anthony. "Boy Culture: Middle-Class Boyhood in Nineteenth-Century America." In *Meanings for Manhood: Constructions of Masculinity in Victorian America,* ed. Mark C. Carnes and Clyde Griffin. Chicago: University of Chicago Press, 1990.

Scheina, Robert L. "The Coast Guard at War." *Commandant's Bulletin* (February 1987): 26–31.

———. "A History of Coast Guard Aviation." *Commandant's Bulletin* (October 1986): 9–43.

Scofield, Kendrick. "No Quarterdeck Dandy Is the Commandant of Revenue Cutter Service." [Place of publication unknown], 16 January 1915.

Shanks, Ralph, and Lisa Woo. *The U.S. Life-Saving Service: Heroes, Rescues and Architecture of the Early Coast Guard.* Petaluma, Calif.: Costaño Books, 1996.

Sims, William Sowden. *The Victory at Sea.* Annapolis: Naval Institute Press, 1984.

Smith, Darrell Heavenor, and Fred Wilbur Powell. *The Coast Guard: Its History, Activities and Organization.* Washington, D.C.: Brookings Institution, 1929.

Some Unusual Incidents in Coast Guard History. U.S. Coast Guard Headquarters, 1950.

"Spotlight On: Coast Guard Headquarters." *Coast Guard Magazine* (May 1957): 23–25.

Stefoff, Rebecca. *The U.S. Coast Guard.* New York: Chelsea House, 1989.

"Stoutest Sailing Ship, *Bear,* 89-Year Winner, Is Down." *Naval Institute Proceedings* 89 (June 1963): 159–62.

Stringer, Harry R., ed. *The Navy Book of Distinguished Service.* Washington, D.C.: Fassett, n.d. Reprint. Planchet Press, 1984.

Strobridge, Truman R., and Dennis L. Noble. *Alaska and the Revenue Cutter Service, 1867–1915.* Annapolis: Naval Institute Press, 1999.

Sweetman, Jack. *The U.S. Naval Academy: An Illustrated History.* Annapolis: Naval Institute Press, 1979.

United States Coast Guard. *Deeds of Valor: From the Annals of the United States Coast Guard.* Washington, D.C.: Government Printing Office, 1943.

———. Public Information Division, Historical Section. *The Coast Guard at War: Alaska.* Washington, D.C.: U.S. Coast Guard Headquarters, 1946.

Van Boskerck, F. S. "The United States Coast Guard: Its Military Necessities." *Naval Institute Proceedings* 45 (April 1919): 623–36.

Wead, Frank W. *Gales, Ice and Men: A Biography of the Steam Barkentine Bear.* New York: Dodd, Mead, 1937.

Westervelt, Frances A. *History of Bergen County, New Jersey, 1630–1923.* 3 vols. New York, 1923.

Wheeler, William J. "Reminiscences of World War Convoy Work." *Naval Institute Proceedings* 55 (May 1929): 385–92.

———. "Reminiscences of 'The Old Guard.'" *U.S. Coast Guard Academy Alumni Association Bulletin* (January–February 1980): 22–25.

Wichels, Ernest D. "Recalling the Day the Great White Fleet Came In." *Vallejo Times-Herald,* 13 April 1980, 5.

Witcover, Jules. *Sabotage at Black Tom: Imperial Germany's Secret War in America, 1914–1917.* Chapel Hill: Algonquin Books, 1989.

Woodward, Clayton W. *History of Bergen and Passaic Counties, New Jersey.* Philadelphia: Everts and Peck, 1882.

~ず Further Reading ず~

History has paid almost no attention to Ellsworth P. Bertholf. Most books about Coast Guard or Revenue-Cutter Service history mention him as one of the three members of the overland relief expedition to Point Barrow in the winter of 1897–98, and usually also mention him as the final commandant of the Revenue-Cutter Service and the first commandant of the Coast Guard. Virtually nothing has been written about the rest of his career or his personal life, perhaps because of the Coast Guard's relative obscurity in American history. Fewer than 270 books have been published about the history of the Coast Guard and its antecedents during the past 211 years, while approximately 500 have been published about the Marine Corps's history, and more than 1,800 have been published about the U.S. Navy during that same period.

Few of Bertholf's personal records survive. The most important source is the small collection of letters and papers at the library of the U.S. Coast Guard Academy, which also holds the papers of several senior officers associated with Bertholf. Shortly after he participated in them, Bertholf wrote two lengthy articles about his two major expeditions. He described his part in the Point Barrow rescue in "The Rescue of the Whalers," published in the June 1899 issue of *Harper's New Monthly Magazine,* and his expedition across Russia in "Expedition to Siberia," published as an appendix in Sheldon Jackson's *Eleventh Annual Report on Introduction of Domestic Reindeer into Alaska* (1902).

There is no biography of Bertholf or any other member of the Coast Guard or its antecedent organizations. The sole biography of a U.S. Coast Guard personality is George F. Foley's 1945 book about a dog, *Sinbad, the Mascot of the Cutter* Campbell.

The best history of the Revenue-Cutter Service during Bertholf's time is Irving King's *The Coast Guard Expands, 1865–1915: New Roles, New Frontiers*. The best history of the Coast Guard's early years is Robert Erwin Johnson's *Guardians of the Sea: History of the United States Coast Guard, 1915 to the Present*.

Although it does not deal with the overland rescue mission, Truman R. Strobridge and Dennis L. Noble's *Alaska and the U.S. Revenue Cutter Service, 1867–1915* provides a good background on the service's Alaskan operations. Dorothy Jean Ray's *The Eskimos of Bering Strait, 1650–1898* argues, not always convincingly, that the importation of reindeer into Alaska was not necessary. Whether or not that is true, America's leaders had only the Inuit people's best interests in mind when they dispatched Bertholf on that humanitarian mission.

ʻ≈ *Index* ≈˘

·~ About the Author ~·

C. Douglas Kroll is an assistant professor of history at the College of the Desert in Palm Desert, California. He graduated from the U.S. Coast Guard Academy in 1971 and served as a Coast Guard officer afloat and overseas before resigning his commission to become a chaplain in the U.S. Navy. He retired in 1996 as a commander in the Naval Reserve Chaplain Corps. He holds a Ph.D. in history from the Claremont Graduate University and is the author of numerous articles on Coast Guard and naval history. Currently he is working on a project dealing with the Imperial Russian Navy in San Francisco during the American Civil War.

The Naval Institute Press is the book-publishing arm of the U.S. Naval Institute, a private, nonprofit, membership society for sea service professionals and others who share an interest in naval and maritime affairs. Established in 1873 at the U.S. Naval Academy in Annapolis, Maryland, where its offices remain today, the Naval Institute has members worldwide.

Members of the Naval Institute support the education programs of the society and receive the influential monthly magazine *Proceedings* and discounts on fine nautical prints and on ship and aircraft photos. They also have access to the transcripts of the Institute's Oral History Program and get discounted admission to any of the Institute-sponsored seminars offered around the country.

The Naval Institute also publishes *Naval History* magazine. This colorful bimonthly is filled with entertaining and thought-provoking articles, first-person reminiscences, and dramatic art and photography. Members receive a discount on *Naval History* subscriptions.

The Naval Institute's book-publishing program, begun in 1898 with basic guides to naval practices, has broadened its scope in recent years to include books of more general interest. Now the Naval Institute Press publishes about one hundred titles each year, ranging from how-to books on boating and navigation to battle histories, biographies, ship and aircraft guides, and novels. Institute members receive discounts of 20 to 50 percent on the Press's more than eight hundred books in print.

Full-time students are eligible for special half-price membership rates. Life memberships are also available.

For a free catalog describing Naval Institute Press books currently available, and for further information about subscribing to *Naval History* magazine or about joining the U.S. Naval Institute, please write to:

Membership Department
U.S. Naval Institute
291 Wood Road
Annapolis, MD 21402-5034
Telephone: (800) 233-8764
Fax: (410) 269-7940
Web address: www.navalinstitute.org